INVENTING THE AUTOMOBILE

Erinn Banting

Crabtree Publishing Company
www.crabtreebooks.com

Crabtree Publishing Company
www.crabtreebooks.com

Coordinating editor: Ellen Rodger
Series and project editor: Adrianna Morganelli
Designer and production coordinator: Rosie Gowsell
Production assistant: Samara Parent
Scanning technician: Arlene Arch-Wilson
Art director: Rob MacGregor
Project development, editing, photo editing, and layout: First Folio Resource Group, Inc.: Tom Dart, Sarah Gleadow, Debbie Smith, Adam Wood
Photo research: Maria DeCambra
Consultants: Ron Barnett, Antique Automobile Club of America; Jack Innes, President, The Canadian Automotive Museum; Tracy Powell, *Automobile Quarterly*
Photographs: ALIX/Photo Researchers, Inc.: p. 28 (top); Justin Allfree/istock International: p. 19 (top); AP/Wide World Photo: p. 22 (top), p. 26 (bottom), p. 29 (top), p. 30 (bottom), p. 31 (top and center); Austrian Archives/Corbis: p. 11; Bettmann/Corbis: p. 10 (top), p. 17; David Caton/Alamy: p. 14; David Cooper/Toronto Star/firstlight.ca: p. 30 (top); Corbis: p. 6 (top); Granger Collection, New York: p. 6 (bottom), p. 7 (top), p. 16 (bottom); George Hall/Corbis: p. 25 (bottom); Hulton-Deutsch Collection/Corbis: p. 5 (bottom), p. 7 (bottom), p. 10 (bottom); Jim Jurica/istock International: p. 18; Helen King/Corbis: p. 19 (bottom); Lester Lefkowitz/Getty Images: p. 25 (top); © 1981 Cindy Lewis: All Rights Reserved.: p. 12; National Motor Museum/HIP/The Image Works: p. 13 (top); National Motor Museum/Topham-HIP/The Image Works: p. 23; Charles O'Rear/Corbis: p. 15; Photodisc/firstlight.ca: p. 24; Reuters/Corbis: p. 28 (bottom); Stapleton Collection/Corbis: p. 5 (top); Karen Town/istock International: p. 26 (top); Tony Tremblay/istock International: p. 22 (bottom); Alex Wong/Getty Images: p. 31 (bottom); David Woods/Corbis: p. 27; Other images from stock photo CD.
Illustrations: Dan Kangas: title page, pp. 20–21; www.mikecarterstudio.com: p. 3, p. 8, p. 9

Cover: The work of early inventors led to the development of the car, which has improved many aspects of people's lives.

Title page: Early and modern cars have many similarities, but cars today are much faster, come in many different models and colors, and have many more features than the first cars.

Contents: Four-stroke internal combustion engines power most cars.

Crabtree Publishing Company
www.crabtreebooks.com 1-800-387-7650

In Canada: We acknowledge the financial support of the Government of Canada through the Book Publishing Industry Development Program (BPIDP) for our publishing activities.

Cataloging-in-Publication Data
Banting, Erinn.
Inventing the automobile / written by Erinn Banting.
p. cm. -- (Breakthrough inventions)
Includes index.
ISBN-13: 978-0-7787-2812-2 (rlb)
ISBN-10: 0-7787-2812-9 (rlb)
ISBN-13: 978-0-7787-2834-4 (pb)
ISBN-10: 0-7787-2834-X (pb)
1. Automobiles--Design and construction--History--Juvenile literature. 2. Inventions--History--Juvenile literature. I. Title. II. Series.
TL147.B243 2006
629.2'3109--dc22 **2005034061**
LC

Published in the United States
PMB 16A,
350 Fifth Ave.,
Suite 3308,
New York, NY
10118

Published in Canada
616 Welland Ave.,
St. Catharines,
Ontario, Canada
L2M 5V6

Published in the United Kingdom
White Cross Mills
High Town, Lancaster
LA1 4XS
United Kingdom

Published in Australia
386 Mt. Alexander Rd.,
Ascot Vale (Melbourne)
VIC 3032

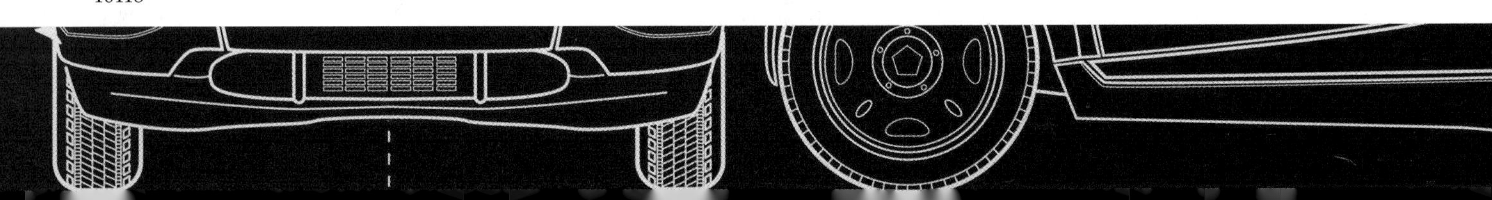

Contents

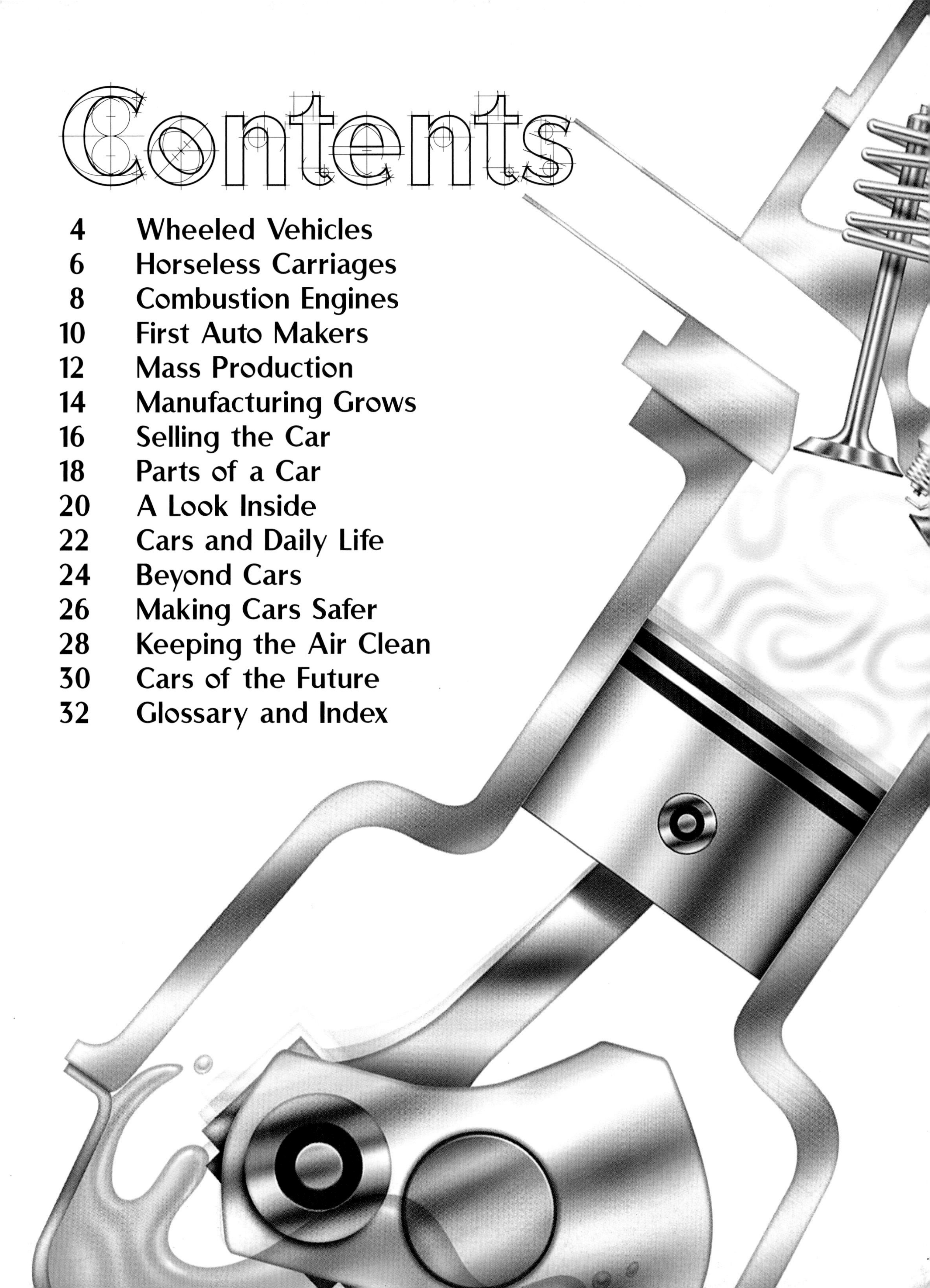

Wheeled Vehicles

The invention of the automobile has had an enormous impact on the world. People drive cars as a means of transportation, they rely on cars for their work, and they enjoy cars as a hobby. Worldwide, manufacturers build more than 30 million cars each year.

Life Before Wheeled Vehicles

Before wheeled vehicles, people traveled over land on foot or on animals, such as camels, horses, oxen, and donkeys. The poor conditions of the few roads made land travel very difficult. Rivers and lakes provided natural routes for rafts, boats, and ships.

On a Roll

The invention of the wheel improved land transportation by making it possible to roll goods over different types of **terrain**. Ancient Chinese drawings suggest the first wheel was built around 8000 B.C. The oldest wheel discovered by **archaeologists** was made around 3500 B.C. in Mesopotamia, which is an ancient region in present-day Iraq.

All methods of early transportation were sometimes dangerous. Watercraft could be damaged in storms, and animals could be injured or die on long journeys.

The language of ancient Rome was Latin. The Latin word for "chariot" is carra*, which is the origin of the word "car."*

Getting Around

People soon began to build carts, which had two wheels, and wagons, which had four wheels. Chariots were two-wheeled vehicles pulled by horses or camels. Fast and easy to steer, chariots transported people in Egypt, Greece, Rome, and India between 3000 B.C. and 1500 B.C., but they were too small to transport supplies.

The most common vehicle used to transport goods during the **Roman Empire** was the *plaustrum*. The *plaustrum* was made from a large plank of wood laid on two or four wheels, and was pulled by oxen.

From Carts to Coaches

During the **Middle Ages**, people in western Europe improved on the cart's design by adding steerable **axles**, which made turning easier. Iron springs and leather belts fastened between the axles and the frame absorbed some of the bumpiness of the ride. Passenger comfort improved with the invention of the coach, a vehicle with an enclosed seating area, pulled by horses.

Carriages were open vehicles that sometimes had fabric tops to protect the vehicles' occupants. People in large cities often hired carriages to take them from place to place.

Horseless Carriages

To improve their speed and durability, early inventors attached steam engines or electric motors to the frames of carriages, which were previously pulled by animals. These early experiments led to the development of the car.

Picking up Steam

Early steam engines were powered by coal or wood. As the fuel burned, water boiled to create steam. The steam expanded, moving the engine and other parts of the vehicle. Nicolas-Joseph Cugnot, a member of the French army, built the first steam-powered vehicle in 1769, called the "steam wagon." It was used to carry large weapons, such as cannon, into battle.

(below) Nicolas-Joseph Cugnot's steam wagon was the first wheeled vehicle to move under its own power, but it had to be stopped every ten minutes to let the engine build up enough steam to keep it moving.

Full Steam Ahead!

European inventors built on Cugnot's work and made engines smaller and more efficient. Their vehicles could travel greater distances before having to stop to build up steam. Some vehicles were difficult to steer and control, which caused accidents, and the boilers, where steam was created, often exploded. Engines also **backfired**, creating loud noises that startled people. In countries such as England, vehicles powered by engines were considered so frightening and dangerous that the government passed laws restricting their use to private roads and property.

(above) Early motorized vehicles were nicknamed "horseless carriages." Many had seats in the front and platforms in the back on which drivers stood so they did not block passengers' views.

Steam Cars

As steam engines improved and as people began to build more cars to carry passengers and goods, cars gained popularity in Europe and North America. In the early 1900s, the De Dion Bouton, built by French mechanics George Bouton and Charles-Armand Trépardoux, was one of the most popular steam cars in Europe. The Stanley Steamer, built by American brothers Freelan and Francis Stanley, was popular in the United States.

(above) The Baker Motor Vehicle Company built electric cars between 1898 and 1916 in the United States.

Running on Electricity

Between 1880 and the early 1900s, electric cars, which were powered by batteries, were introduced in England, Europe, and North America. Electric cars did not backfire like steam cars, and they were less expensive to power, but they could only travel 50 miles (80 kilometers) before their batteries needed recharging. This made them inconvenient to use for long journeys.

(below) Steam-powered road locomotives, found mainly in England in the 1800s and early 1900s, towed wagons or carriages that held goods and passengers.

Combustion Engines

To further improve a vehicle's speed and efficiency, many inventors experimented with internal combustion engines, which are powered by burning a mixture of air and gasoline within cylinders. The success of their experiments forever changed the car.

The Internal Combustion Engine

American inventor Samuel Morey designed one of the first internal combustion engines in the early 1800s. He received a **patent** for the engine in 1826, but never built one that worked well. The internal combustion engine burned fuel, such as kerosene or turpentine. When the fuel was heated and mixed with air, it combusted, or exploded, in a chamber at the top of the cylinder. This created pressure that caused a piston to move up and down inside the cylinder. The piston's movement pushed the mixture of fuel and air through the cylinder to power the engine. It also pushed **exhaust** out of the cylinder.

The Two-Stroke Engine

In 1859, Belgian-born inventor Étienne Lenoir built the first internal combustion engine that powered a car. It operated on two strokes, which are upward or downward movements of the piston. In 1863, Lenoir built a car around one of his engines, but the engine was not powerful enough to make the car run reliably.

A Modern Two-Stroke Engine

Here is how a modern two-stroke engine works:

Stroke 1: The piston moves down, pushing exhaust out of the cylinder and pulling in a mixture of fuel and air.

Stroke 2: The piston moves up, compressing the mixture of fuel and air. A **spark plug** fires and ignites the mixture, and the explosion pushes the piston back down.

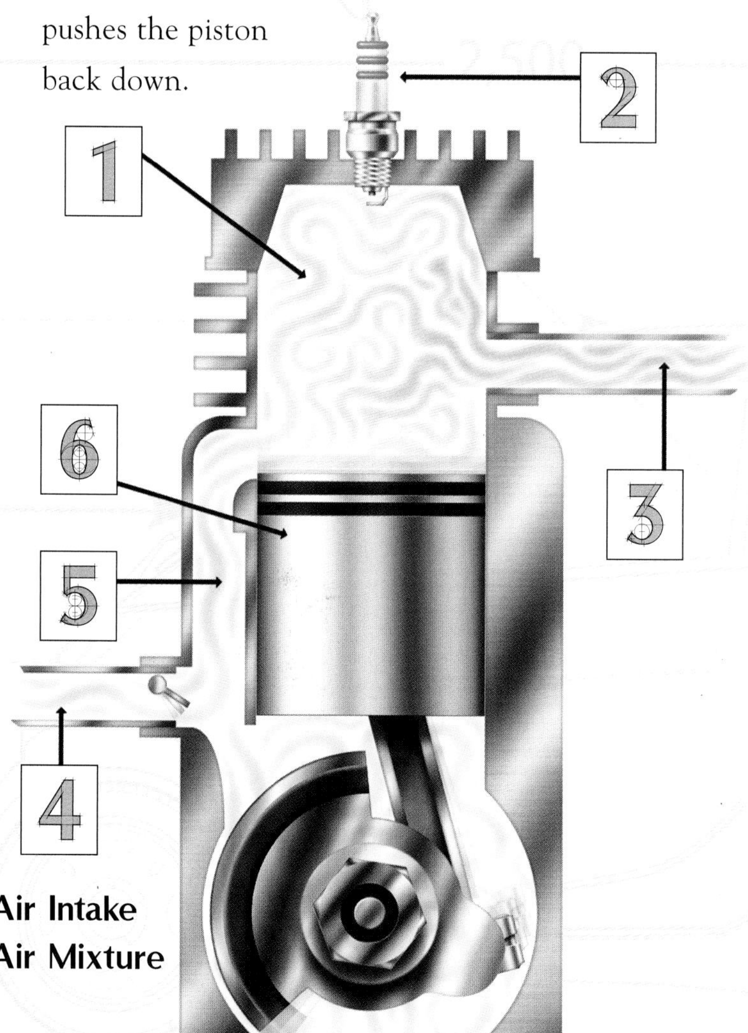

1. Combustion Chamber
2. Spark Plug
3. Exhaust Outlet
4. Fuel and Air Intake
5. Fuel and Air Mixture
6. Piston

The Four-Stroke Engine

German engineer Nikolaus Otto, with his partners Gottlieb Daimler and Wilhelm Maybach, built the first working four-stroke engine in 1876. The four-stroke engine was much easier to run than the two-stroke engine and was able to power a vehicle successfully.

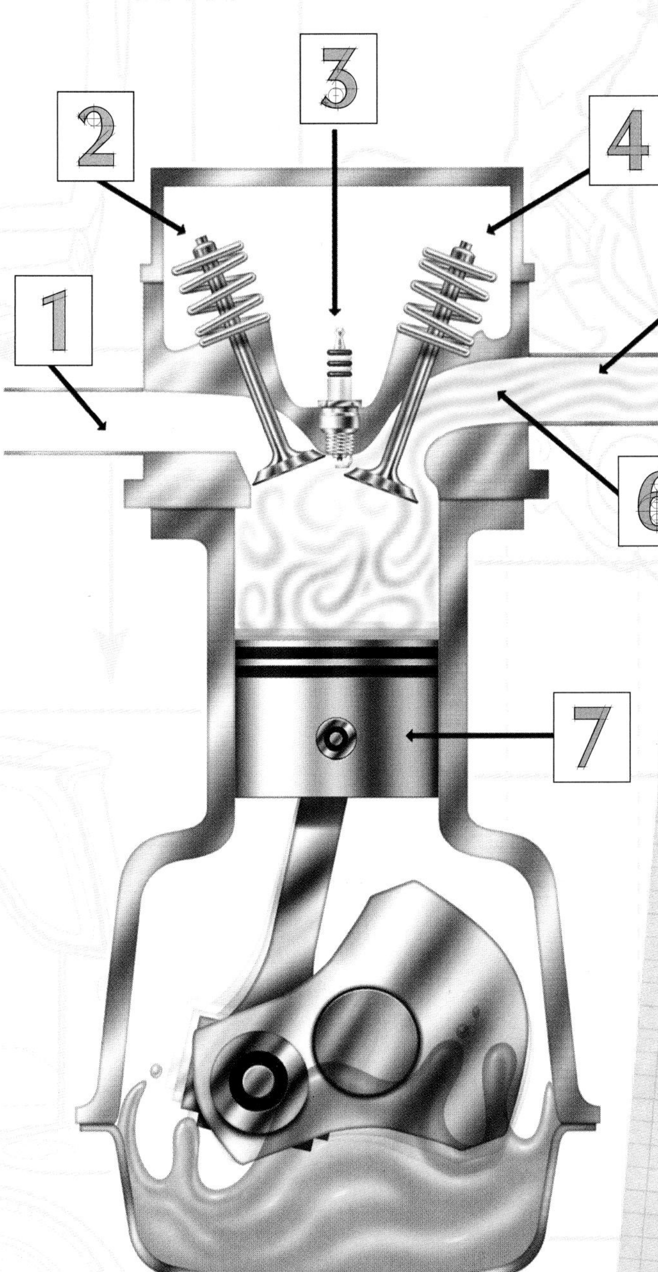

A Modern Four-Stroke Engine

Here is how a modern four-stroke engine works:

Stroke 1: The piston pushes down, pulling a mixture of fuel and air into the cylinder.

Stroke 2: The piston moves up, compressing the mixture at the top of the cylinder.

Stroke 3: A spark from the spark plug ignites the mixture, and the pressure caused by the explosion pushes the piston down.

Stroke 4: The piston is forced back up to release the exhaust.

1. Exhaust Outlet
2. Exhaust Valve
3. Spark Plug
4. Intake Valve
5. Fuel and Air Intake
6. Fuel and Air Mixture
7. Piston

Patent Controversy

Disputes over patents happened regularly when the first cars were built. Nikolaus Otto is considered the first person to build a four-stroke internal combustion engine, but French engineer Alphonse Beau de Rochas had already patented the idea in 1862 — 14 years before Otto built his engine. In 1886, after more than 30,000 engines had been built based on Otto's model, Otto's right to de Rochas's patent was revoked, or taken back, and Otto was forced to pay de Rochas a percentage of the money he earned from the engines he sold.

First Auto Makers

In the late 1800s and early 1900s, the main goal of people developing cars was to make vehicles that actually worked. As a result of their experimentation, technology changed so quickly that new models became obsolete, or outdated, soon after they were introduced.

Karl Benz

German engineer Karl Benz built a motorized tricycle that was powered by a four-stroke internal combustion engine in 1885. The tricycle, called the *Motorwagen*, reached speeds of up to eight miles (13 kilometers) per hour.

(above) Karl Benz's Motorwagen ***had one of the earliest braking systems. Leather straps tightened around the*** hubs ***of the wheels to make them slow down or stop.***

(above) Gottlieb Daimler and Wilhelm Maybach's first vehicle reached speeds of up to 12 miles (19 kilometers) per hour.

Daimler and Maybach

In 1886, German engineers Gottlieb Daimler and Wilhelm Maybach attached a four-stroke engine to the back of a carriage frame, and created the first workable car. The driver sat at the front and steered the vehicle with a **tiller**. The vehicle also had a four-speed gearbox. The gears helped move the wheels faster without increasing the speed of the engine, which prevented the engine from overheating or exploding. To shift gears, drivers had to stop their cars and then start them again to continue their journeys.

Daimler-Benz

In 1890, Daimler and Maybach founded the Daimler Motor Company. They introduced the Mercedes, a line of cars still built today. The Mercedes had many new features, including radiators, which helped cool engines, and smaller steel frames, which made the cars lighter so they traveled more quickly. In 1926, the Daimler Motor Company joined Karl Benz's company, Benz & Co., to form Daimler-Benz. Daimler-Benz built the first **diesel** car in 1936. Its engine, invented by Rudolph Diesel in 1890, was more powerful and efficient than other types of engines.

Panhard-Levassor

French engineers René Panhard and Emile Levassor built their first car in 1891. The vehicle was powered by a Daimler engine placed under the hood at the front, not in the back as in earlier cars. Four years later, they introduced the first **transmission** with a clutch, in their Panhard car. For the first time, drivers could change gears while the car was still moving.

Workers at the Daimler Motor Company paint cars in this photograph from 1904. Today, the company is known as Mercedes-Benz.

Mass Production

As the demand for cars increased, the number and size of auto plants in Europe and North America grew. Factories improved the manufacturing process, making it faster and less expensive to build cars. With these changes, cars became more affordable for the average person.

The Assembly Line

Early cars were built one at a time and entirely by hand. The assembly sometimes took more than a year, which made cars very expensive and affordable only to the wealthy. In 1901, American automobile manufacturer Ransom Eli Olds installed an assembly line in his auto plant, Olds Motor Works. Workers moved from car to car to install a piece or system, which sped up the manufacturing process. Olds also began using parts built by other manufacturers, instead of having his factory manufacture all the parts. After introducing these changes, production costs decreased and car production increased.

Henry Ford

When Henry Ford founded the Ford Motor Company in 1903, his goal was to build cars that were affordable, mechanically reliable, and long lasting. In 1913, Ford introduced the first moving assembly line at his factory in Dearborn, Michigan. Workers no longer had to move from car to car to add their parts. Instead, the cars traveled to the workers along conveyor belts. Ford's moving assembly line allowed workers to build a car in 93 minutes, compared to the days, or even weeks, other car manufacturers required. Reducing the time it took to build cars and increasing production lowered the cost of cars.

One of the first widely sold cars in the United States was the curved-dash Oldsmobile, manufactured by Olds Motor Works.

(above) Between 1908 and 1927, Ford's assembly line built more than 15 million cars.

(below) Early Ford models were named after letters of the alphabet. Ford's first popular car was the Model T, built between 1908 and 1928.

Shift Work

Demand for cars increased as the prices of cars decreased. To keep up with the demand, Henry Ford divided the workday into a day shift and a night shift. Each shift used different employees. This way, Ford's manufacturing plants could build cars into the night without exhausting workers. Ford also doubled the average salary he paid his workers compared to workers in other car factories. Ford's changes improved conditions for workers in other industries as well, who argued that they wanted to be treated as well as employees of Ford.

Manufacturing Grows

Once assembly lines became common, many more car manufacturers became profitable. Car manufacturing grew to be one of the largest industries in the world. Many car manufacturers that opened in the early 1900s still build cars today.

BMW

German manufacturer BMW was formed in 1916 as Bayerische Flugzeugwerke, a company that made aircraft engines. By 1928, BMW was building cars that became known for their high speed and **endurance**. Today, BMW manufactures luxury and sports cars, as well as motorcycles, under its own name and under the names of companies it has purchased. These include the luxury car manufacturer Rolls-Royce.

With the introduction of the electric starter, Cadillac sales climbed from 10,000 in 1911 to 14,000 in 1912.

General Motors

In 1908, an American businessman named William Crapo Durant created a car company called General Motors (GM) by buying many small- and medium-sized car companies, including Olds Motor Works. GM introduced new features to cars, including electric starters, which debuted in the 1912 Cadillac. Electric starters replaced the cranks, or handles, that people had to use to start their cars. Today, GM manufactures cars under lines such as Cadillac, Buick, Pontiac, Chevrolet, Saturn, and Hummer.

1769 Nicolas-Joseph Cugnot builds the first steam vehicle.

1876 Nikolaus Otto builds the first four-stroke internal combustion engine.

1890 Rudolph Diesel patents the diesel engine.

1901 The assembly line is first used.

1908 Electric headlights are first installed on cars.

1912 The electric starter is introduced in GM's Cadillac.

1928 Brakes on all four wheels become standard on most cars.

Chrysler

Walter P. Chrysler took over the Maxwell Motor Company factory in 1923 and, the following year, renamed it the Chrysler Corporation. Over the next 80 years, the Chrysler Corporation grew to be one of the largest car manufacturers in the United States. Among its most influential innovations was the minivan, introduced in 1984. Minivans, which have extra seats and room in the interior to make passengers more comfortable, are a popular mode of transportation for families. In 1998, Chrysler merged with Daimler-Benz and became Daimler-Chrysler.

Modern assembly lines use robots to do many of the tasks that people once did. Robots increase the efficiency of factories, enabling them to build more cars.

Toyota

The Toyota Motor Corporation was established in Japan in 1933, and became one of the country's largest car manufacturers in the 1960s and 1970s. Toyota's efficient, compact engines burned much less fuel than other cars at the time. The company's later innovations include a **hybrid** car called the Prius, which is more fuel-efficient than other types of cars.

Honda

The Honda Motor Company, established in 1946, began as the Honda Technical Research Institute. The Japanese company built small, efficient internal combustion engines, and, later, motorcycles and cars. The cars, made with **fiberglass** bodies, were lightweight and **aerodynamic**, so they moved faster than many other cars at the time.

1940 The first cars with automatic transmissions are built.

1954 The first robot is installed on a U.S. assembly line.

1964 Seat belts become mandatory in all cars.

1973 Air bags are introduced.

1984 The minivan is introduced.

1997 The first commercially successful hybrid car is sold in Japan.

2004 The smart fortwo car is introduced in North America.

Selling the Car

Early manufacturers tried many strategies to convince people to buy cars. They advertised in newspapers, held car races to attract public interest, and improved the performance, style, comfort, and safety of automobiles.

On Your Mark! Get Set! Go!

Car races gave manufacturers a way to test and display their new models and inventions, and they were exciting for spectators. During the first car race, which was held on public roads in 1894, 102 contestants raced between Paris and Rouen, in France. Beginning in 1927, Italian car manufacturers, such as Lancia, Alfa Romeo, Maserati, and Ferrari, entered their cars in the Mille Miglia, a race through Italy's mountains that began and ended in Rome.

(above) The Indy 500 is one of the most popular car races today. More than 250,000 spectators visit Indianapolis, in the United States, to watch the race each year.

(below) In this photograph from the 1920s, a driver races against an airplane. Races with airplanes demonstrated the speed that cars could reach.

The Indy 500

Danger to spectators, racers, and livestock caused public road races to decrease in number. In 1908, American businessman Carl G. Fisher began building the first U.S. racetrack in Indianapolis. Three years later, more than 80,000 spectators came to watch the first race. It was known as the Indy 500: "Indy" because it took place in Indianapolis and "500" because drivers had to race 500 miles (805 kilometers), which was 200 laps around the track.

Feeling Comfortable

Beginning around 1913, many companies began building cars with interiors that were elaborately decorated in wool, silk, and **ivory**. They hoped that the added comforts would increase sales. Over time, other features were added to make cars more comfortable and enjoyable to drive, including heating and air conditioning systems, radios, and CD and DVD players.

Sales of cars also increased with additional safety features. Windshields, bumpers, rearview mirrors, and locks were offered as optional features, and are now standard on all cars. Newer safety features include car alarms and global positioning system (GPS) devices, which show drivers their positions on the road and suggest the best routes to reach their destinations.

Dynamic Obsolescence

Between the early 1920s and late 1940s, world events such as the **Great Depression** and **World War II** made it difficult for car manufacturers to stay in business. To ensure his company did not go bankrupt, GM president Alfred P. Sloan came up with an idea he called dynamic obsolescence. Each year after a car was introduced, GM improved the design of the vehicle, until it became obsolete. Sloan argued that the changes made cars look better and run more smoothly. His critics accused Sloan of making people feel that they had to buy the latest cars, which would result in GM earning more money. In spite of the criticism, other car manufacturers soon adopted Alfred P. Sloan's idea.

An advertisement for a car by the R-C-H Corporation lists the features and improvements to passenger safety, comfort, and price.

Parts of a Car

Many parts, including the engine, lubrication system, fuel system, transmission, and brakes, work together to help a car run. The first cars had fewer than 50 parts, while cars today have thousands.

The Engine

The engine is the most important part of the car. Today, most cars are powered by gas engines, while many construction vehicles, trucks, and some automobiles are powered by diesel engines. Diesel engines use diesel fuel, a cheaper and less refined fuel than gasoline. Diesel fuel burns slightly longer than gasoline and creates more power. Some vehicles are powered by hybrid engines, which rely on a combination of sources, such as gasoline and battery-powered motors. Hybrid engines are more fuel-efficient than other types of engines.

Transmission

Cars have either manual or automatic transmissions. In a car with a manual transmission, the driver uses a clutch and gearshift to change gears. An automatic transmission shifts gears automatically, depending on how fast or slow the car is being driven. When a car reaches the maximum speed for a particular gear, the transmission shifts into a higher gear. When a car slows down, the transmission shifts into a lower gear.

(above) A car's lubrication system oils metal parts so they do not wear out quickly. The oil needs to be changed approximately every 4,000 miles (6,000 kilometers).

Fuel System

In early cars, gravity helped move fuel from the fuel tank to the engine. When driving uphill, cars often stopped because the fuel could not reach the engine. Cars had to be turned around, so the fuel tanks were above the engines, and driven in reverse. Modern cars rely on fuel-injection systems to suck the right amount of fuel from fuel tanks, mix it with air, and inject it into the engines' cylinders.

(right) Gears help cars reach maximum speeds using minimum power.

Brakes

There are two main kinds of brakes. Drum brakes are large drums, or cylinders, with metal blocks, called brake shoes, inside. They fit in cars' wheels. When the brake pedal is pressed, the brake shoes push against the inside of the drums, slowing or stopping the wheels. Disc brakes are like the brakes on a bicycle. When a driver presses on the brake pedal, calipers, which are like clamps, squeeze against discs. This slows down or stops the wheels.

A mechanic fixes a car's brakes. Many cars today have antilock brakes. Antilock brakes prevent the wheels from locking up when a driver slams on the brakes, so that the car does not skid on wet or slippery roads.

A Look Inside

A car's exterior consists mainly of a body, wheels, windows, and lights. Inside, cars are made up of thousands of parts that help them run smoothly and safely.

1. Battery: The battery supplies power to the car's starting system, computer, lights, and all other electric parts. An alternator keeps the battery charged.

2. Ignition switch: Turning the key in the ignition switch unlocks the steering wheel and sends electrical power to most of a car's accessories, such as the lights and radio. Turning it further feeds electrical power to the starting system, so the car can start.

3. Accelerator pedal: The accelerator pedal sends a message to the fuel-injection system, letting the car know how much fuel needs to be burned for it to run at different speeds.

4. Steering wheel: Turning a steering wheel in an older car required a lot of effort. Power steering, introduced in 1951, made steering faster and more accurate.

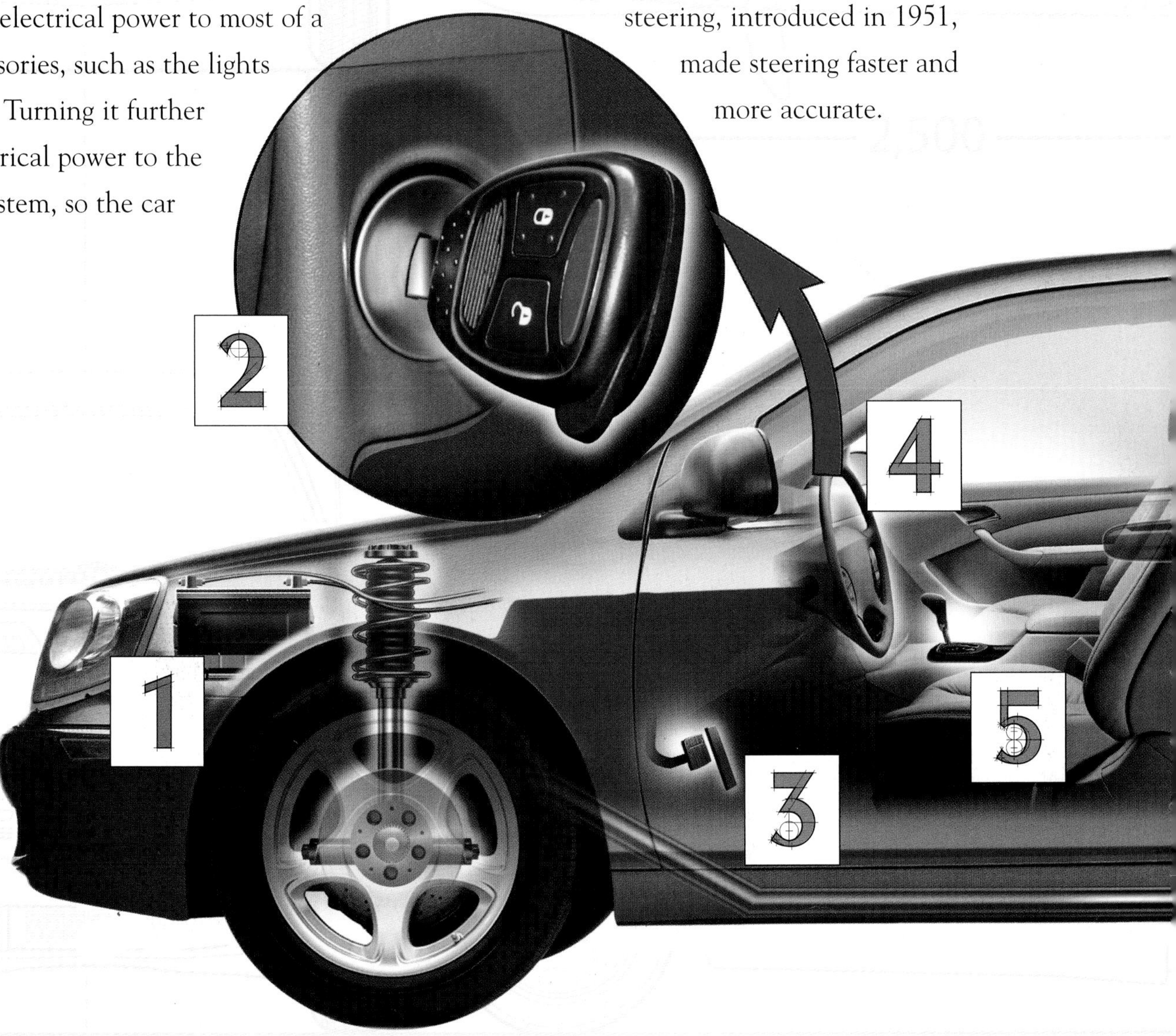

2

4

1

5

3

5. Shift lever: In a car with an automatic transmission, the shift lever allows the driver to shift from "Park" into "Reverse," "Neutral," or "Drive." It also allows a driver to move into first or second gear when going up or down steep slopes, to prevent the engine from overworking, or the brakes from wearing out too quickly.

6. Muffler: Mufflers help absorb noise made by the exhaust. A pipe leading from the muffler directs the exhaust out the back of the car.

7. Body: Most car bodies are made of steel, with trim made of plastic. The roof, rear, and sides of the car are usually reinforced with extra steel framework pieces, which better protect the vehicle's occupants during a collision.

8. Tires: Tires transfer power from the engine to the road. Different tires have **treads** designed to operate over different road surfaces and conditions.

9. Suspension system: The two main parts of the suspension system are the springs and the shock absorbers, or shocks. The springs allow wheels to move over bumps without causing the rest of the car to move too much. The shocks keep the car from bouncing when it hits a bump.

10. Lights: Exterior lights, including headlights, taillights, brake lights, and signal lights, help drivers see roads and other cars at night. They also indicate to other drivers whether cars are slowing down, stopping, or turning.

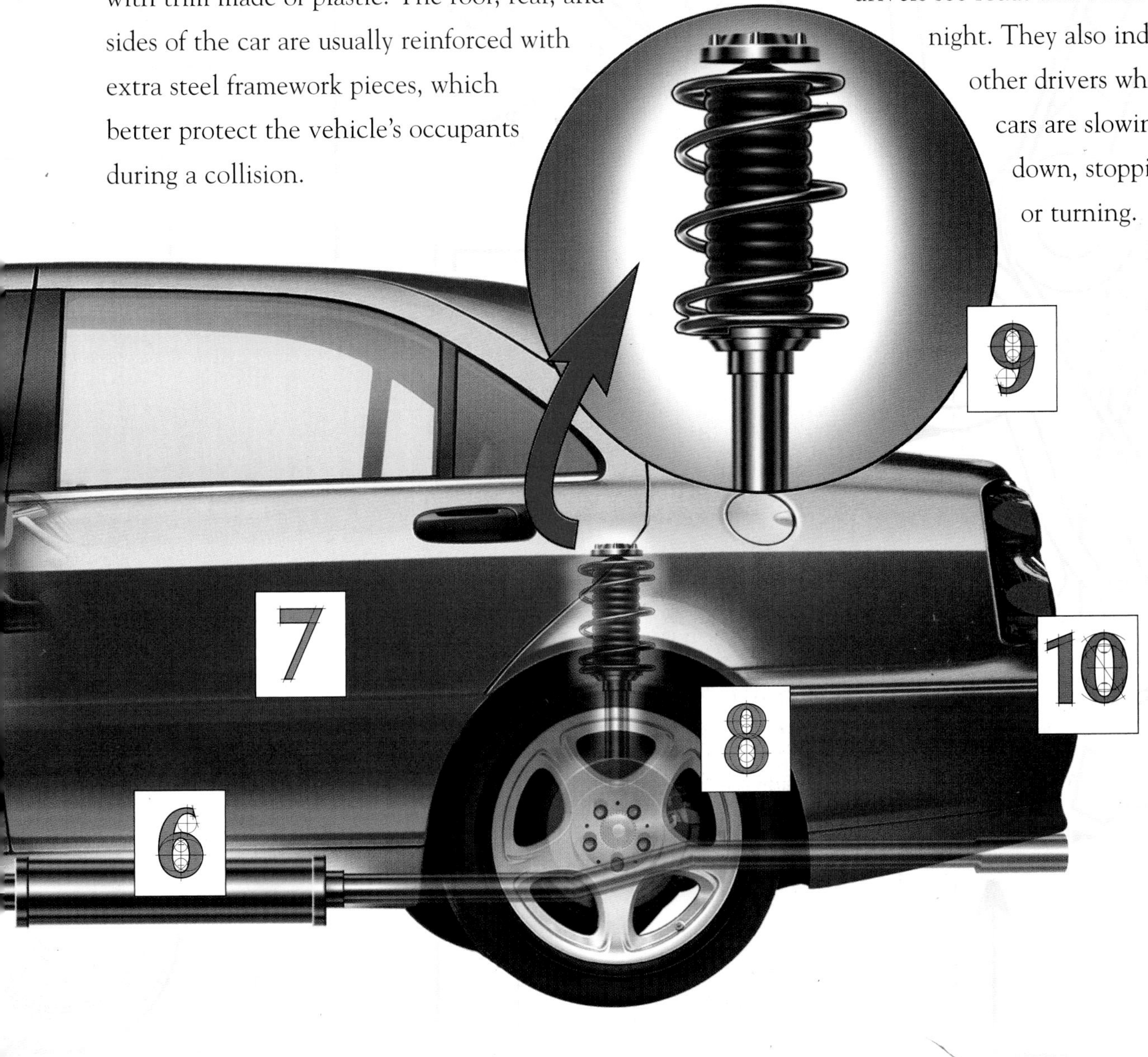

9

7

10

8

6

Cars and Daily Life

Today, people rely on cars on a daily basis. Their widespread use has changed the way roads and cities are built, created new industries, and led to thousands of laws that protect drivers and pedestrians.

Riding the Roads

Early roads were made of dirt or were covered in cobblestones or gravel. When cars became more common, paved roadways, which were safer and lasted longer, were built. The first paved roadways were constructed in England with layers of stone chips and tar rolled flat. Today, many roads are made with a mixture of tar and gravel.

Highways

Highway surfaces are often made of concrete, which is more durable than tar and gravel. Highways were first built in European countries such as Germany and Italy in the 1930s. The roads, which connected major cities, had higher speed limits and multiple lanes that could hold more traffic. By the 1940s, the United States, Canada, and England also built highways. As highways developed, cities and suburbs grew because people could live farther away from where they worked.

(above) Car clubs organize events that bring together people who want to buy, repair, sell, share stories, or learn more about particular types of cars.

(left) In the United States, people drive more than 1.3 trillion miles (2.09 trillion kilometers) each year, which equals more than one billion trips around the world.

In the early 1900s, when cars did not have roofs or sides, women wore wide-brimmed hats with veils and men wore large goggles and hats to protect themselves from wind, rain, snow, or strong sunshine.

New Industries

The popularity of cars has allowed other industries to grow. Millions of manufacturers build parts for cars, including bodies, engines, and tires. Service stations, which began as small roadside sheds, sell gas, perform minor repairs, and sell beverages, snacks, and other items people need while traveling. Other companies publish maps, manufacture games that children play during car trips, design advertisements for roadside billboards, or sell **insurance** to drivers.

Laws for Drivers

As the number of cars on roads increased, new laws were needed to protect pedestrians and drivers. England's Red Flag Law was one of the earliest traffic laws. Until 1904, the Red Flag Law required a driver to have a person carry a red flag in front of the car to warn others that a vehicle was approaching. Today, traffic laws regulate everything from who can drive to how fast they can drive.

Beyond Cars

The success and popularity of cars paved the way for other means of land transportation. Today, a wide range of vehicles is built, and vehicles are modified for specific needs.

A Variety of Vehicles

Car manufacturers have introduced vehicles such as minivans, recreational vehicles (RVs), and sport-utility vehicles (SUVs) to meet the needs of their customers. Minivans give drivers more room to transport their families safely and comfortably. RVs, which include sleeping quarters, washrooms, and kitchens, are used for camping. SUVs are combinations of cars and four-wheel drive trucks. They have a lot of room for passengers and equipment, and can be easily driven in mud, in snow, or on rough terrain.

Adapted Vehicles

Many cars, vans, and buses can be adapted so that people with disabilities are able to drive and ride in them. Minivans can be equipped with ramps for easier access, and the floors can be lowered so that people in wheelchairs can drive from their chairs. Hand controls replace accelerator and brake pedals in vehicles whose drivers have limited use of their legs. Power steering can be adjusted so that it is easier for people with limited movement in their hands to steer.

Automated ramps on public buses make it easier for people with disabilities to board and exit.

Delivery Trucks

Before the early 1900s, horse-drawn wagons delivered groceries and supplies from local farms and factories to people's homes. Today, goods are delivered by transport trucks, which have special features to ensure the items they carry arrive safely. Many trucks have ramps to help with loading and unloading, and bars to keep goods from moving. Trucks that carry animals have openings so that fresh air can circulate, as well as drinking facilities and space to store animal feed. "Sleeper" trucks are built with beds, televisions, and toilets so that drivers can rest during long journeys.

(right) Transport trucks load and unload their cargo. Trucks transporting food that must be refrigerated or frozen have *insulated* ***floors, walls, and ceilings to keep food from spoiling.***

Emergency Vehicles

Before cars were invented, doctors, firefighters, and police traveled to people's homes on foot, by horse, by horse-drawn carriage, or by bicycle. These early forms of transportation were slow and often did not arrive in time. Today, vehicles such as police cars, ambulances, and fire engines are used for emergencies.

Police cars are modified so that they can be driven faster than other vehicles in emergency situations. They have more powerful engines and brakes, and very efficient transmission, suspension, and cooling systems. Ambulances are designed to have room in the back for two or more patients, and for emergency medical technicians (EMTs) or paramedics to care for them. Ambulances also carry equipment and supplies for emergency care, and sometimes, light rescue equipment.

Fire engines are equipped with tanks that have water and foam for extinguishing fires. They also have hoses, water pumps, and pump panels, used to control which hoses have water flowing through them, and how much.

Making Cars Safer

Early cars did not have many of the safety features that today's cars have, such as turn signals, mirrors, bumpers, and shatterproof glass. In addition to these features, cars today are built with crumple zones, seat belts, and air bags to protect drivers and passengers in case of collisions.

The Seat Belt

Seat belts, first installed by Nash Motors in 1949, are one of the most important safety features of cars today, but they were not mandatory in cars until the mid-1960s. Early seat belts crossed over people's hips, which held them in their seats during collisions, but did not prevent their heads from hitting dashboards or windshields. In 1959, Nihls Bolin, an engineer at Swedish car manufacturer Volvo, invented the three-point seat belt. A three-point seat belt has one strap across the lap and a second diagonal strap across the chest to better hold passengers in place.

(above) In many parts of the world, it is illegal to be in a car without a seat belt.

Crumple Zones

In 1959, Bela Berenyi, an engineer at Mercedes-Benz, introduced crumple zones in the front and rear of most of the company's cars. These zones absorb the shock of a collision and crumple so that passengers are not injured. Berenyi also improved side impact beams, which absorb the shock if cars are hit on the side.

(below) Crumple zones, along with the use of stronger materials, reduce the risk of injury during a collision.

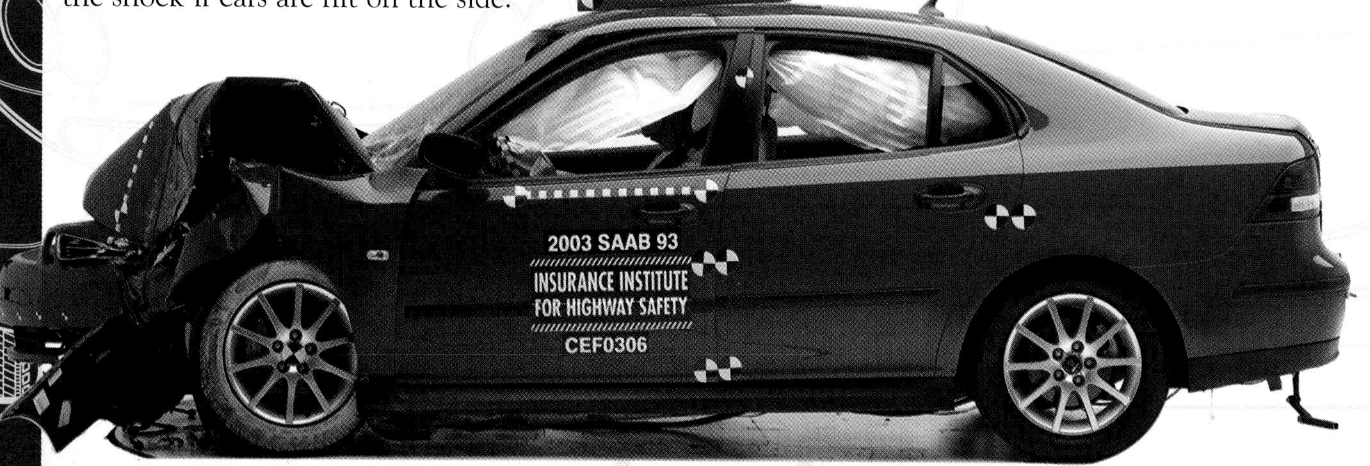

Air Bags

In 1952, American inventor John Hetrick developed the idea for air bags, which are safety cushions built into steering wheels, dashboards, doors, and seats. When cars are hit head-on or on the sides, the air bags inflate and reduce the impact of crashes on drivers and passengers. Early air bags sometimes harmed a vehicle's occupants because they inflated so quickly and with such force. Today, with the help of computers, air bags deploy to different sizes at different speeds, depending on the severity of the crash.

Car Seats

The first child car seats, invented in the 1930s, held children still while cars were moving, but did not protect them in collisions. In 1960, designers at Volvo improved the car seat by adding two diagonal belts that held children in place, and prevented them from being thrown forward in collisions. Volvo later designed a seat that faced backward, further protecting children during head-on collisions.

Crash Tests

To test how safe cars are, manufacturers perform safety tests, or crash tests. Early crash tests were performed in the 1930s to measure the damage done to cars when they crashed at different speeds. In the 1950s, crash test dummies were added to safety tests to see what impact collisions had on human beings. Today, there are crash test dummies made to the height and weight of the average man, woman, child, and even dog.

Cars are given crash test scores. Five stars indicate the most protection, one star the least.

Keeping the Air Clean

Cars have improved many aspects of people's lives, but they have also threatened the environment. They use up natural resources, cause pollution, and fill landfill sites. Car manufacturers are looking for ways to reduce the damage, and commuters help by taking public transit or car pooling.

Alternative Fuels

Scientists and car manufacturers are experimenting with alternative ways of powering cars. Biodiesel and ethanol are fuels made from plants, which are **renewable** resources. They release fewer harmful emissions than gasoline. In some major cities, diesel buses are being replaced with buses that use fuel cells. Fuel cells mix gasoline, natural gas, propane, methanol, or other **hydrogen**-rich fuels with oxygen, and convert the mixture to electricity and heat. Water is the only emission from a fuel cell. Car manufacturers are also developing improved hybrid cars.

(above) Cyclists in large cities often wear anti-pollution masks to protect themselves from vehicle emissions.

(right) Battery-powered electric cars, which were popular in the early 1900s, are being built again because they produce very little pollution. Some shopping malls have outlets where drivers of electric cars can recharge their vehicles' batteries.

The World Solar Challenge is a 1,870-mile (3,010-kilometer) car race that takes place in Australia every other year. Solar-powered cars have panels on their roofs that use the sun's energy to charge their batteries. The batteries then supply power to the engines.

Problems with Pollution

The emissions, or pollutants, released by cars, and the **Freon** used in cars' air-conditioning systems, contribute to air pollution and the **greenhouse effect**. Many countries have passed strict emissions laws. Older cars must be tested regularly for excess emissions of carbon monoxide and other harmful gases. Cars that fail the test must have their exhaust systems and engines adjusted before the vehicles can be driven again.

Recycling Helps

In the past, tires, metal, and plastic from scrapped cars have gone into garbage dumps and landfill sites. Recently, programs have been developed to encourage recycling. Rubber tires are shredded into small chips and turned into asphalt, which is used to pave roads. Cars are shredded into small pieces, which are separated into glass, steel, plastic, rubber, and chemicals. These materials are individually recycled or made into new parts for cars. Harmful substances, such as **antifreeze**, battery acid, brake fluid, and oil, which can seep into the soil and enter waterways, are removed before cars are recycled.

Plastic, used in a car's interior, can take up to 100 years to decompose, or break down. Aluminum, used on the car's exterior and in its engine, can take up to 300 years.

Cars of the Future

Concept cars, nicknamed "dream cars," are prototypes **that are built using the latest technology and designs. Automakers use them to demonstrate innovations in car design and to measure the public's reaction to new features.**

The smart fortwo ▸

Mercedes-Benz introduced the smart fortwo car in Europe in 1998 and in North America in 2004. The car, which seats two people, is only eight feet (2.5 meters) long and five feet (1.5 meters) wide. Originally designed for crowded city streets, smart fortwo cars are so small they can be parked either beside the curb or facing it. The car's three-cylinder diesel engine is also extremely fuel-efficient.

◂ The Jeep Treo

The Jeep Treo was introduced in 2004. The car looks small on the outside, but is roomy enough for a driver and two passengers, one in the front and one in the back. Two wings on the back of the car contain the rear lights and vents that help cool the car.

Toyota PM ▸

The Toyota PM, which stands for Personal Mobility, was introduced in 2003. The PM seats one person, and does not have side doors. The driver enters through a hatch that holds the bubble-shaped windshield. When the hatch closes, the seat reclines to make the ride more comfortable.

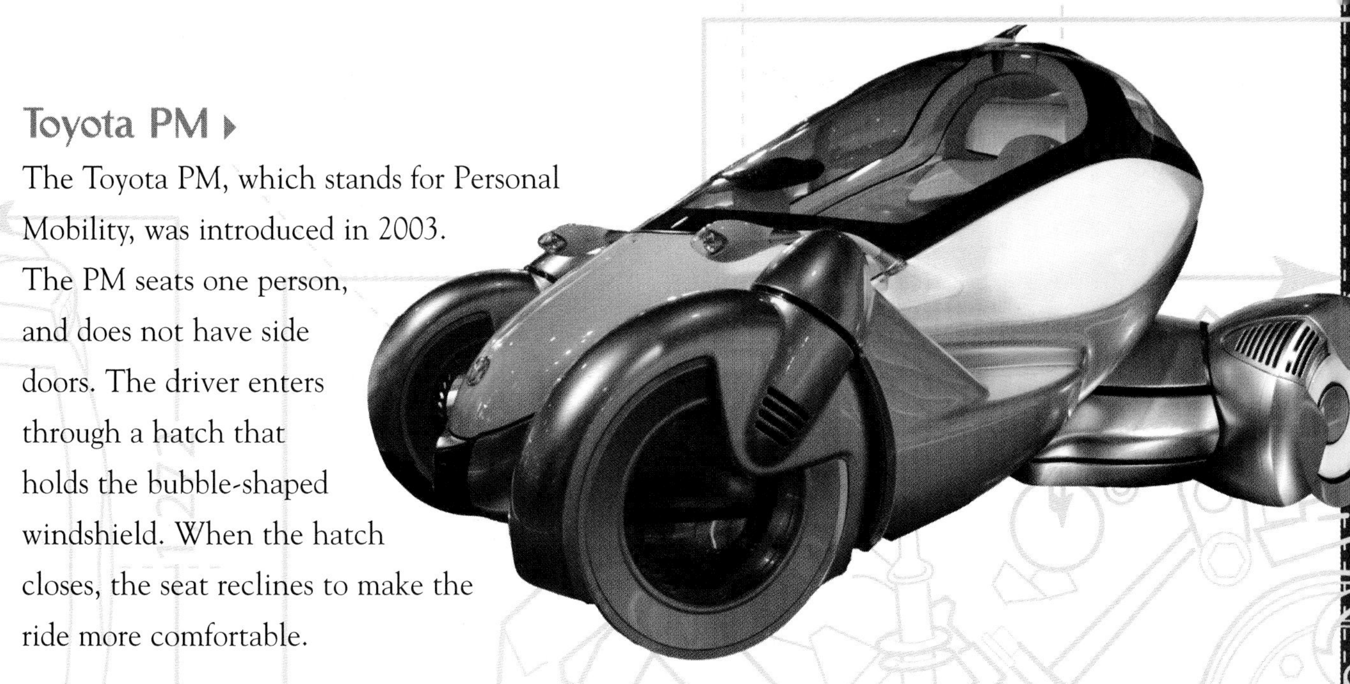

◂ The Lotus Elise

Introduced as a compact sports car in 1995, the Lotus Elise is only 12.5 feet (3.8 meters) long. Made with aluminum, a lightweight metal, it is one of the fastest sports cars for a car its weight, able to accelerate to more than 100 miles per hour (185 kilometers per hour) in just 13.5 seconds.

The Mercedes-Benz Bionic ▾

Mercedes-Benz looked to science and nature for their 2005 Bionic concept car. Engineers built the car frame based on the bone structure of the boxfish, a tropical fish that moves quickly through water despite its boxy shape. Lightweight, aerodynamic, and powered by a diesel engine, the car is 20 to 30 percent more fuel efficient than other cars of similar size.

Glossary

aerodynamic Designed with round edges to move more easily through strong winds

antifreeze A liquid added to a car's cooling system to allow it to operate in low temperatures

archaeologist A person who studies the past by examining buildings and artifacts

axle A long bar on which wheels turn

backfire To explode and make a loud noise, such as when fuel ignites too soon

cylinder The chamber in which a piston moves

diesel A type of fuel that is ignited by heat from compressed air, rather than by an electrical spark

endurance The ability to remain in good working condition over a period of continued use

exhaust Fumes and gases that are released as fuel is used up

fiberglass A material made from glass fibers, or threads

Freon A chemical compound used in refrigeration and air conditioning systems

Great Depression A period of mass unemployment and poverty in the 1930s

greenhouse effect The warming of the Earth's surface due to pollution in the atmosphere

hub The central part of a wheel

hybrid A vehicle whose engine uses more than one source of power

hydrogen A colorless, odorless gas

insulate To prevent heat from entering or leaving an area by surrounding it with a special material

insurance Money paid to a driver in the event of a collision or theft, to compensate for damages

ivory A white bone-like substance from the tusks of animals such as elephants

Middle Ages The period from about 500 A.D. to 1500 A.D. in western Europe

natural resource A material found in nature, such as oil or coal

patent A legal document that prevents people from using inventors' ideas for a certain period of time without giving them proper recognition and payment

prototype The first full-size, usually working model of an invention

renewable Able to be used continuously without running out

Roman Empire A group of territories under the control of Rome from 27 B.C. to 395 A.D.

spark plug A device that produces a spark to ignite the fuel mixture in a gasoline engine

terrain The features of land in a particular area

tiller A handle used to steer

transmission Gears and other car parts that transmit, or send, power from the engine to the wheels

tread The part of a tire that touches the road

World War II A war fought by countries around the world from 1939 to 1945

Index

1 2 3 4 5 6 7 8 9 0 Printed in the U.S.A. 5 4 3 2 1 0 9 8 7 6

Put any picture you want on any state book cover. Makes a great gift. Go to www.america24-7.com/customcover

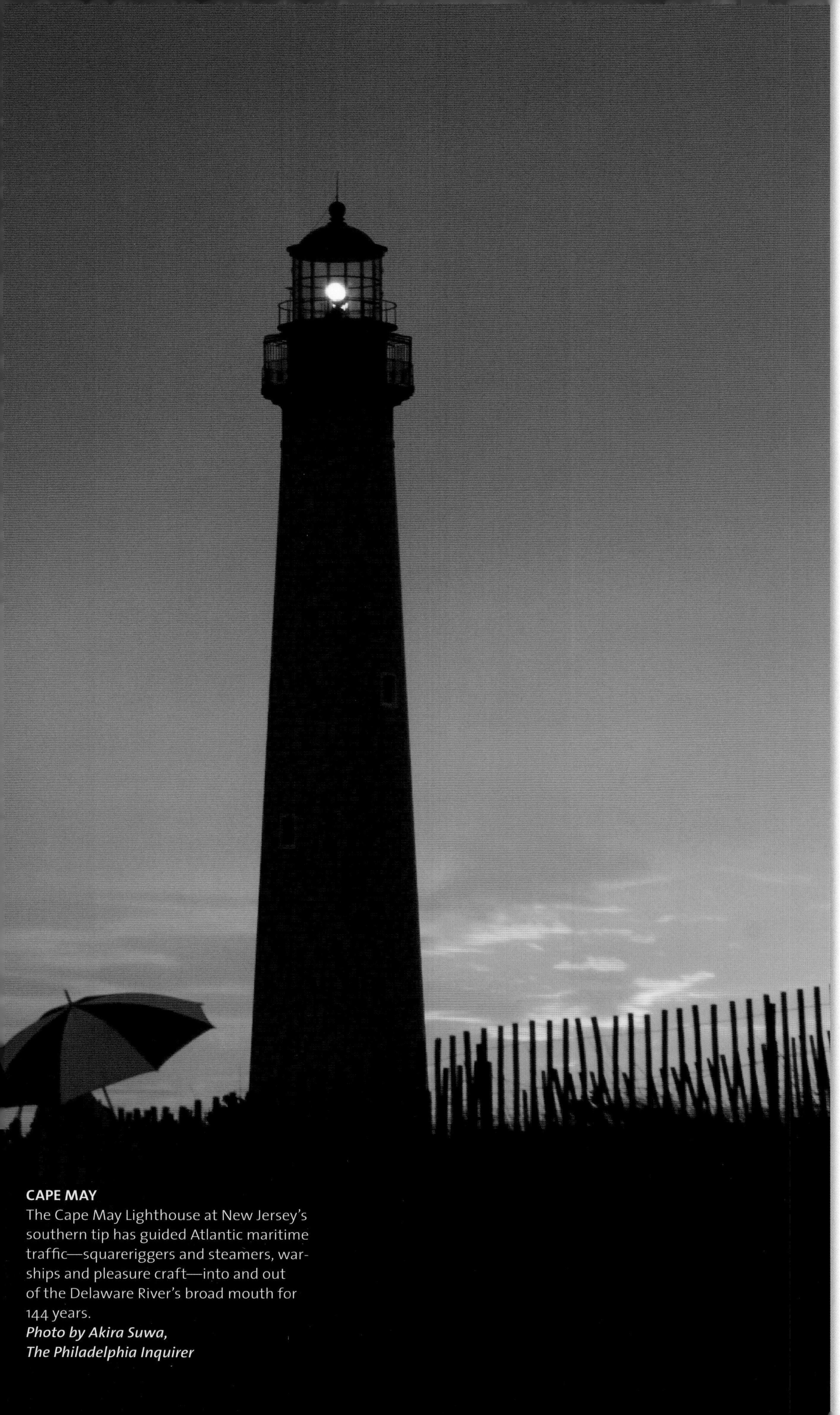

CAPE MAY
The Cape May Lighthouse at New Jersey's southern tip has guided Atlantic maritime traffic—squareriggers and steamers, warships and pleasure craft—into and out of the Delaware River's broad mouth for 144 years.
Photo by Akira Suwa, The Philadelphia Inquirer

New Jersey 24/7 is the sequel to *The New York Times* bestseller *America 24/7* shot by tens of thousands of digital photographers across America over the course of a single week. We would like to thank the following sponsors, the wonderful people of New Jersey, and the talented photojournalists who made this book possible.

OLYMPUS

jetBlue AIRWAYS

Google

DIGITAL POND

DK

LONDON, NEW YORK, MUNICH, MELBOURNE, and DELHI

Created by Rick Smolan and David Elliot Cohen

24/7 Media, LLC
PO Box 1189
Sausalito, CA 94966-1189
www.america24-7.com

First Edition, 2004
04 05 06 07 08 10 9 8 7 6 5 4 3 2 1

Published in the United States by
DK Publishing, Inc.
375 Hudson Street
New York, NY 10014

Cataloging-in-Publication data is available from the Library of Congress
ISBN 0-7566-0070-7

Printed in the UK by Butler & Tanner Limited

First printing, October 2004

JERSEY CITY
Fisherman Mike Cheng casts into the fog on the Hudson River. Behind him rises what will be the tallest building in New Jersey, the 42-story Goldman Sachs Building at Paulus Hook, a formerly neglected riverfront district in Jersey City.
Photo by Thomas E. Franklin

New Jersey 24/7

24 Hours. 7 Days.
Extraordinary Images of
One Week in New Jersey.

Created by Rick Smolan and David Elliot Cohen

DK Publishing

About the America 24/7 Project

A hundred years hence, historians may pose questions such as: What was America like at the beginning of the third millennium? How did life change after 9/11 and the ensuing war on terrorism? How was America affected by its corporate scandals and the high-tech boom and bust? Could Americans still express themselves freely?

To address these questions, we created *America 24/7*, the largest collaborative photography event in history. We invited Americans to tell their stories with digital pictures. We asked them to shoot a visual memoir of their lives, families, and communities.

During one week in May 2003, more than 25,000 professionals and amateurs shot more than a million pictures. These images, sent to us via the Internet, compose a panoramic yet highly intimate view of Americans in celebration and sadness; in action and contemplation; at work, home, and school. The best of these photographs, more than 6,000, are collected in 51 volumes that make up the *America 24/7* series: the landmark national volume *America 24/7*, published to critical acclaim in 2003, and the 50 state books published in 2004.

Our decision to make *America 24/7* an all-digital project was prompted by the fact that in 2003 digital camera sales overtook film camera sales. This technological evolution allowed us to extend the project to a huge pool of photographers. We were thrilled by the response to our challenge and moved by the insight offered into American life. Sometimes, the amateurs outshot the pros—even the Pulitzer Prize winners.

The exuberant democracy of images visible throughout these books is a revelation. The message that emerges is that now, more than ever, America is a supersized idea. A dreamspace, where individuals and families from around the world are free to govern themselves, worship, read, and speak as they wish. Within its wide margins, the polyglot American nation manages to encompass an inexplicably complex yet workable whole. The pictures in this book are dedicated to that idea.

—Rick Smolan and David Elliot Cohen

American nightlight: More than a quarter of a billion people trace a nation with incandescence in this composite satellite photograph.
Photo by Craig Mayhew & Robert Simmon, NASA Goddard Flight Center/Visions of Tomorrow

Jersey: The Best Is in Between

By Dore Carroll

Enough with the *Sopranos* image already. We all know there's more to New Jersey than highway exits, trash dumps, and oil tanks, despite the view from Newark airport.

We have woodlands and mountains, sandy beaches, and ocean waves. We live in cities with theaters and fine restaurants, and in small towns with rich histories. We pray in temples, churches, and mosques, and speak many different languages.

The Garden State nickname is not a joke. South Jersey farmers grow perfect tomatoes and mouthwatering peaches. They sell Jersey Fresh sweet corn in bushels at roadside farm stands and harvest enough cranberries to fill the nation's supermarket shelves with gallons of juice.

An hour's drive from any subdivision reveals forest trails along the Delaware River, bike paths through the Pinelands, and crashing Atlantic surf all along the sandy coast.

The state may be sandwiched between New York and Philly and plagued with shopping malls and traffic jams. But New Jersey has the best of city life and country escapes, beach towns, and shipping ports.

Jerseyans shop in New York City, root for the Giants or Jets, and go to the theater.

Growing up in Bayonne, a blue-collar city with a small-town spirit, my family took day trips "to the city" and vacations "down the shore." We drove past the belching refinery on the Turnpike, fascinated by the labyrinth of pipes and tanks because our father worked there.

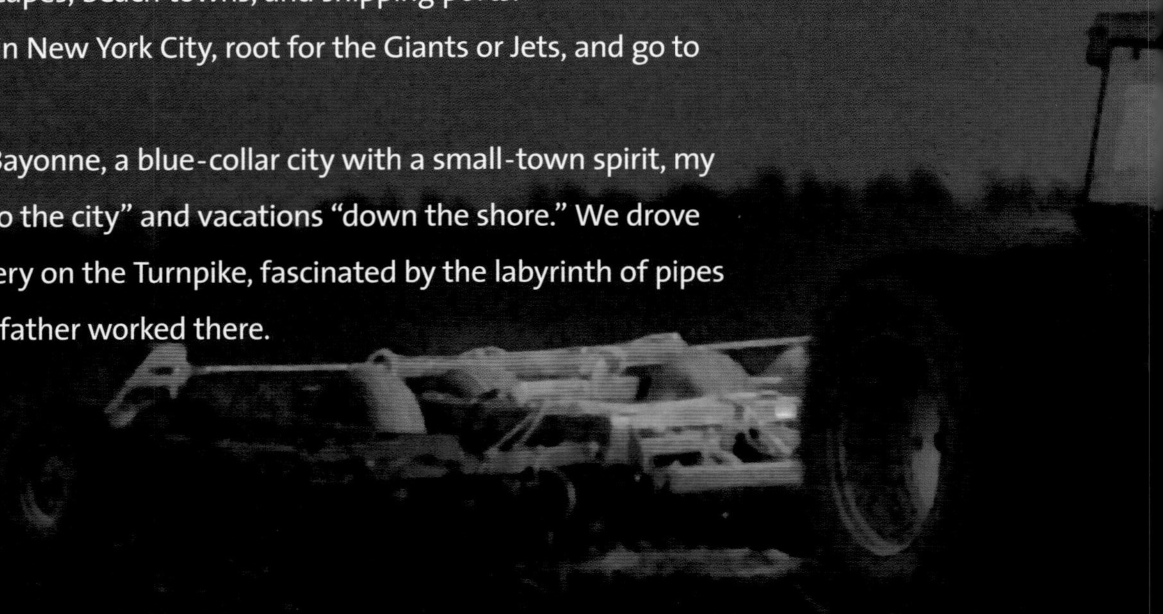

CLINTON TOWNSHIP
A farmer plows his fields in the western hinterlands. The state is a great barrel, said Abraham Browning of Camden in 1876, paraphrasing Benjamin Franklin. It's "filled with good things to eat and open at both ends, with Pennsylvanians grabbing from one end and New Yorkers from the other." New Jersey is the Garden State, Browning said, popularizing the term.
Photo by Ed Murray

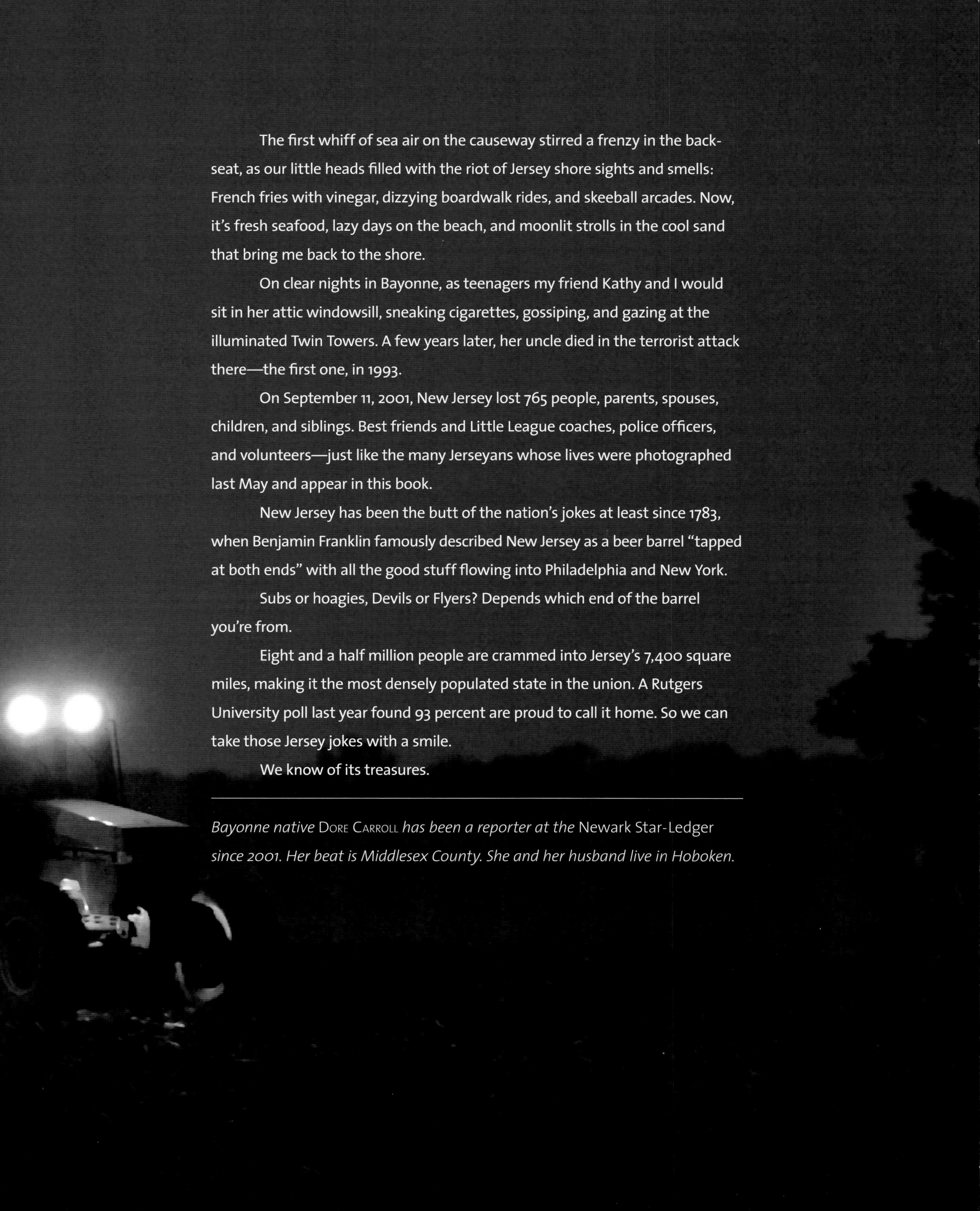

The first whiff of sea air on the causeway stirred a frenzy in the backseat, as our little heads filled with the riot of Jersey shore sights and smells: French fries with vinegar, dizzying boardwalk rides, and skeeball arcades. Now, it's fresh seafood, lazy days on the beach, and moonlit strolls in the cool sand that bring me back to the shore.

On clear nights in Bayonne, as teenagers my friend Kathy and I would sit in her attic windowsill, sneaking cigarettes, gossiping, and gazing at the illuminated Twin Towers. A few years later, her uncle died in the terrorist attack there—the first one, in 1993.

On September 11, 2001, New Jersey lost 765 people, parents, spouses, children, and siblings. Best friends and Little League coaches, police officers, and volunteers—just like the many Jerseyans whose lives were photographed last May and appear in this book.

New Jersey has been the butt of the nation's jokes at least since 1783, when Benjamin Franklin famously described New Jersey as a beer barrel "tapped at both ends" with all the good stuff flowing into Philadelphia and New York.

Subs or hoagies, Devils or Flyers? Depends which end of the barrel you're from.

Eight and a half million people are crammed into Jersey's 7,400 square miles, making it the most densely populated state in the union. A Rutgers University poll last year found 93 percent are proud to call it home. So we can take those Jersey jokes with a smile.

We know of its treasures.

Bayonne native DORE CARROLL *has been a reporter at the* Newark Star-Ledger *since 2001. Her beat is Middlesex County. She and her husband live in Hoboken.*

BAY HEAD
Equidistant from New York City, Philadelphia, and Atlantic City, the resort colony of Bay Head was developed after the Civil War for city folk seeking fresh air.
Photo by Brian Smiga, Preclick

MONTCLAIR
Volunteering at the YMCA for 70 years, George Gimbel, 85, estimates he's taught 2,100 adults to swim. "When someone's afraid, I ask them to try anyway," he says. "Usually, they find they can do it." The retired General Foods engineer swims one-third of a mile before each class and also teaches lifeguarding, ice safety, CPR, and first aid.
Photo by Mia Song, The Star-Ledger

NEW LISBON
One hundred and fifty years ago, this verdant Atlantic White Cedar swamp was cleared to supply firewood for the furnaces of the Lebanon Glass Works. Today the Brendan T. Byrne State Forest offers protection for 35,000 acres of south central Jersey woodlands.
Photo by Dennis McDonald, Burlington County Times

FRANKLIN
Alex Kovach's father painted the historic Bennington Flag on the side of the family's barn for the 1976 American Bicentennial. According to Revolutionary War folklore, a Vermont militia called the Green Mountain Boys carried the flag when they defeated German mercenaries known as the Hessians in the Battle of Bennington on August 16, 1777.
Photo by James W. Anness

VOORHEES
Polliwogs unite: Shanee Thornton, 11, and her cousin Riaa Redd, 8, head to the showers after swimming lessons at the Voorhees YMCA. Shanee likes swimming so much that she has a pool party at a local hotel every year for her birthday.
Photo by Sarah J. Glover, The Philadelphia Inquirer

CLIFTON
Michael Hicks loves animal books. He also likes to grab his photographer mom's camera and muck around in his toy kitchen, taking after his dad, a professional chef. As much as the 21-month-old mimics his parents though, his mom Najlah says, "We're not pushing him in either direction. We just want him to be happy."
Photo by Najlah Feanny

Hearth & Home

SADDLE BROOK
You can run from the law but you can't hide. Michael Hicks, 21 months, is about to find that out as cousin "Sheriff" Matthew Hicks, 3, prepares a sneak attack in the backyard of his Bergen County home.
Photo by Najlah Feanny

HACKENSACK
With the help of his Uncle John, one of 40 guests at his 4th birthday party, Sean Franklin goes in for a slam dunk.
Photo by Thomas E. Franklin

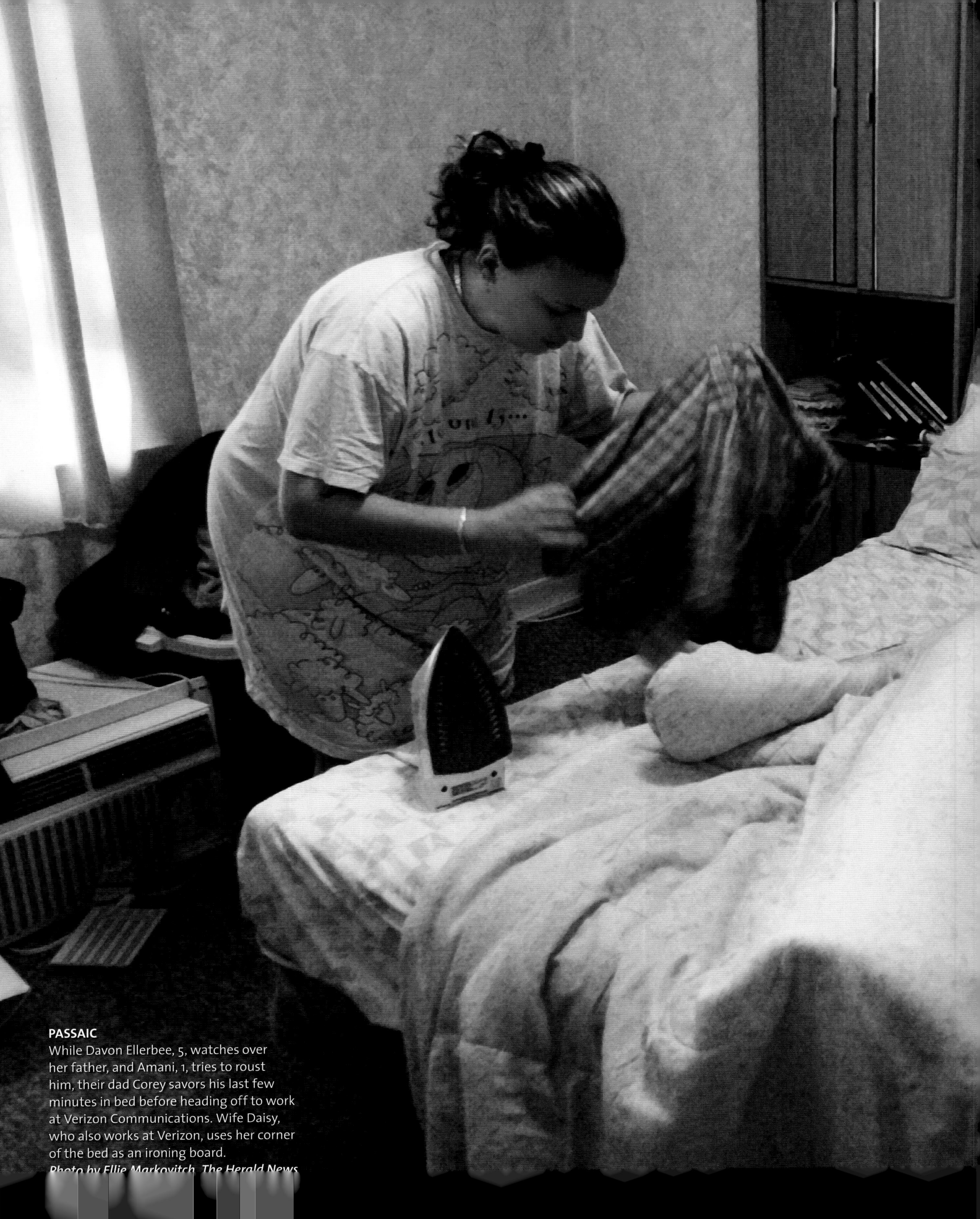

PASSAIC
While Davon Ellerbee, 5, watches over her father, and Amani, 1, tries to roust him, their dad Corey savors his last few minutes in bed before heading off to work at Verizon Communications. Wife Daisy, who also works at Verizon, uses her corner of the bed as an ironing board.
Photo by Ellie Markovitch, The Herald News

6:58

CHERRY HILL

Elaine and Charles DePrince adopted Mia, 8, of Sierra Leone in 1999. They had never expected to adopt. But two of their five sons, both hemophiliacs, died from AIDS a year apart. Their son Michael-Noah, then 14, had seen a TV commercial about the plight of children in war-torn Sierra Leone. Before he died, he asked his parents to help them.

Photos by April Saul

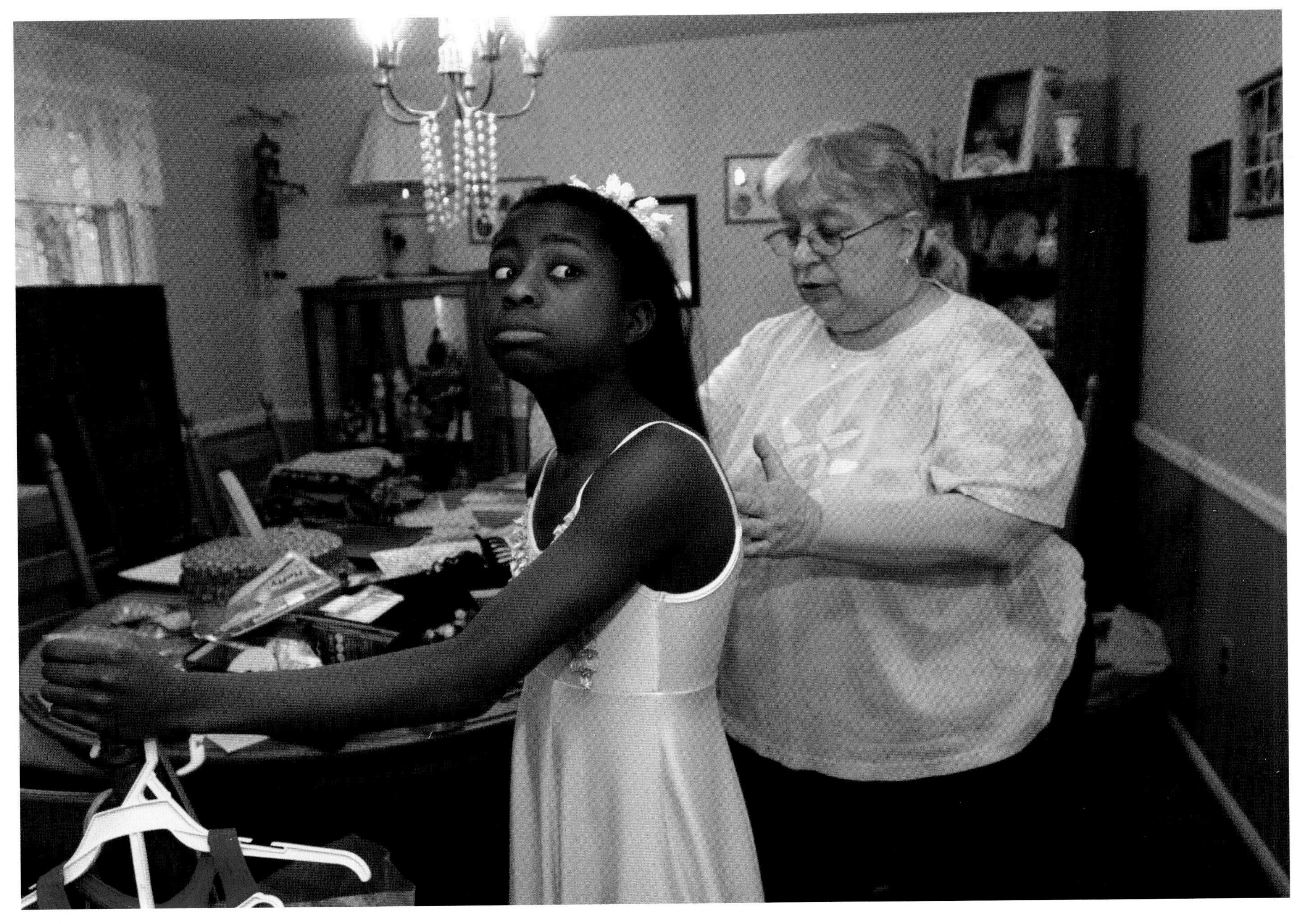

CHERRY HILL

Mariel, 8, is one of three girls adopted from Sierra Leone by the DePrince family. "The adoption wasn't hard because children there are not in great demand," says Elaine DePrince. "The hard part was getting out of Sierra Leone safely."

VOORHEES

A patrol officer, Nichele Vaughan was trained to be self-reliant. So when contractions woke her up before dawn, Vaughn took her older son to her mother's house and drove herself to the Virtua West Jersey Hospital. Ten hours later, second son Cole was born. Sister Loray Vaughan, (second from left) and sister-in-law Correta Smith celebrate the joyous moment.

Photo by Akira Suwa, The Philadelphia Inquirer

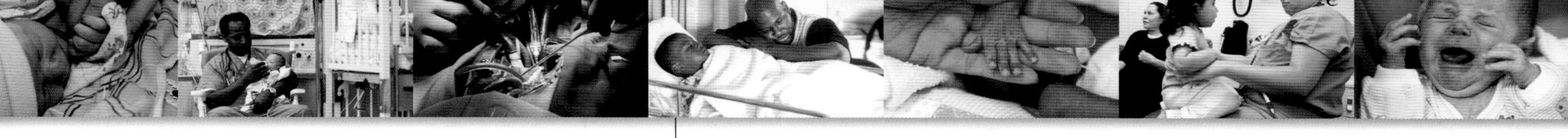

BROWNS MILLS
Vaughn Gaines's son DeVaughn Whitfield, 5, was born with a 1.4-centimeter hole in his heart. At the Deborah Heart and Lung Center, DeVaughn awaits open-heart surgery in which doctors will seal the cavity with a Goretex patch. Five days after the two-hour surgery, DeVaughn returned home in good health.
Photo by Dennis McDonald, Burlington County Times

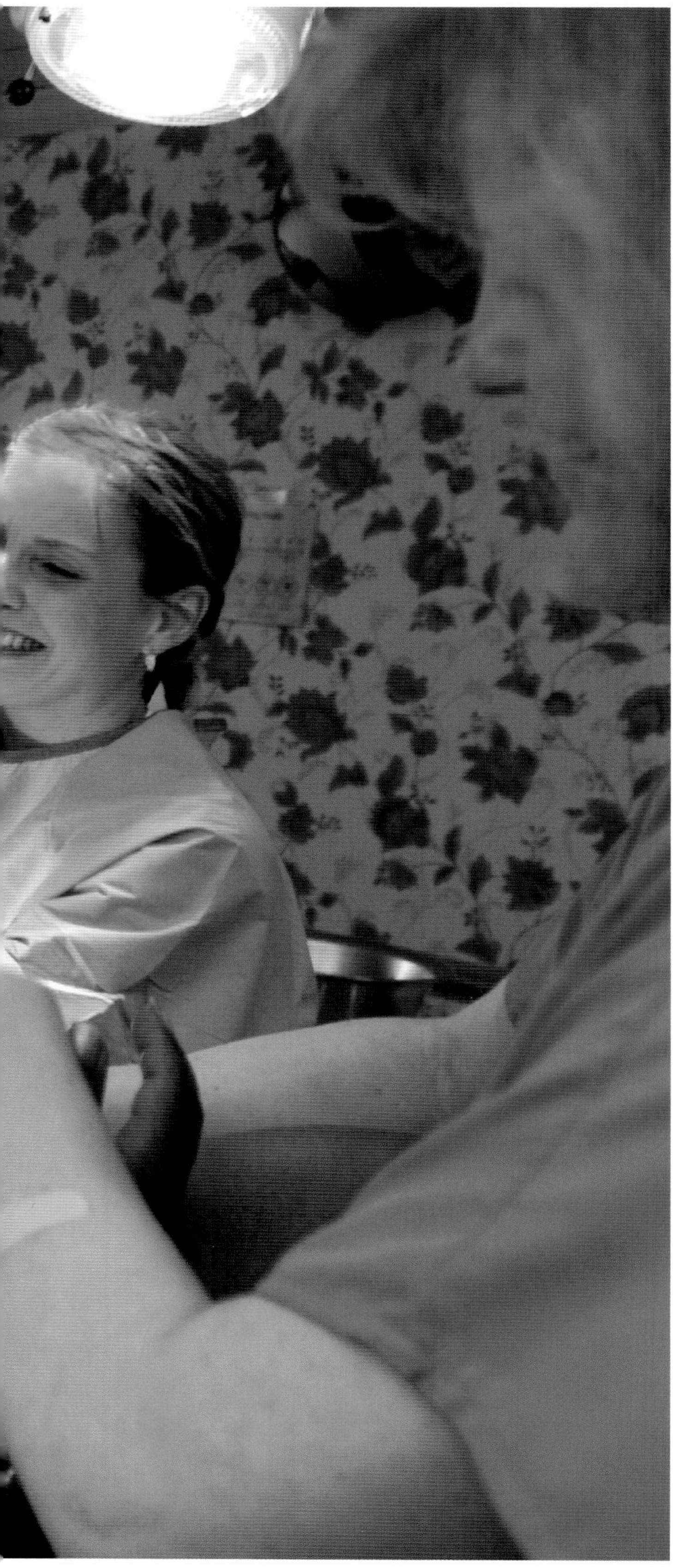

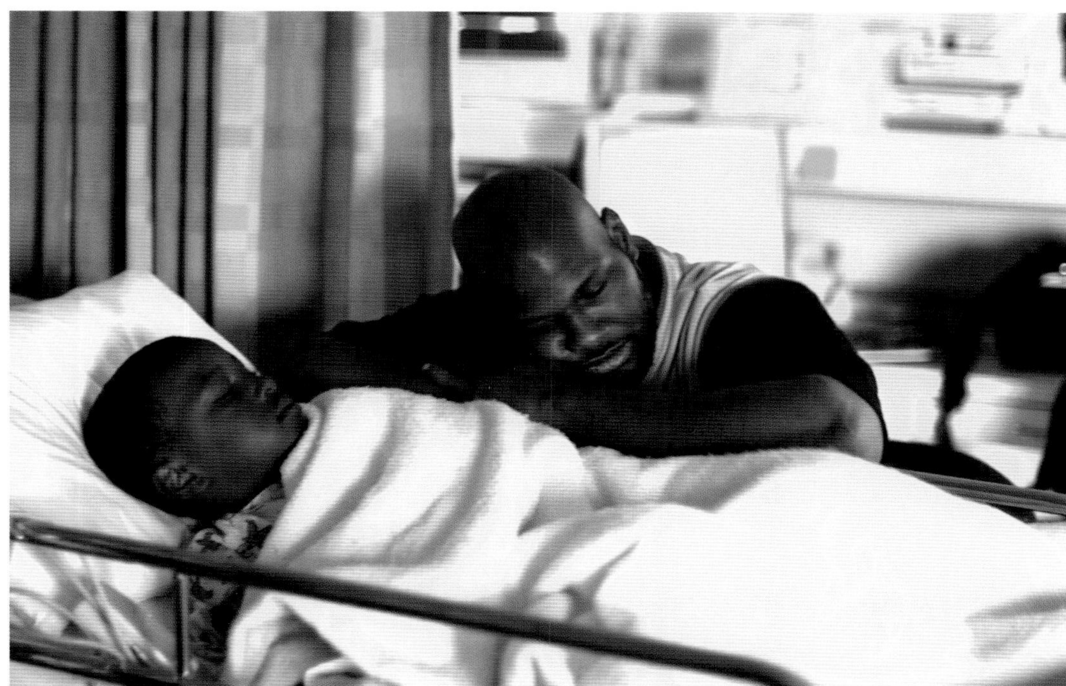

PALISADES PARK
In the small flower shop tucked under a staircase at the Rodeo Plaza Mall, shop manager Yoo-Jin Gim serves lunch to daughter Fiona, 4, and husband H. Won Gim. During the past decade, Palisades Park has evolved from a working-class Italian suburb to a thriving Korean community.
Photo by James W. Anness

VOORHEES
Tuesday McDonald, 5, named after actress Tuesday Weld, displays her artistic bent on the walls of her bedroom. A fan of the Powerpuff Girls, Tuesday likes to act out different characters from her favorite movies, *Lilo & Stitch* and *Finding Nemo*. "I guess she's kind of turned into her name," says her mother Elizabeth.
Photo by Dennis McDonald, Burlington County Times

BEACHWOOD
With eight children, the cleaning is never done. Cindy Davison, 46, grabs time while 20-month-old Gabriella Grace naps. Gabriella is the third disabled child adopted by the Davisons. She has Cornelia de Lange syndrome, which leads to retardation, heart problems, and brain seizures. The Davisons also have five biological children, ages 15 to 26.
Photos by Peter Ackerman, Asbury Park Press

BEACHWOOD
Davison gets help folding laundry from her 11-year-old daughter Hannah. The Davison's first child, Emmy Sue, was born with severe disabilities and died from kidney failure when she was 3. Fourteen years later, after raising five healthy kids of their own, Cindy and her husband Ernie wanted to help another special-needs child, so they adopted Hannah, who has Down's syndrome.

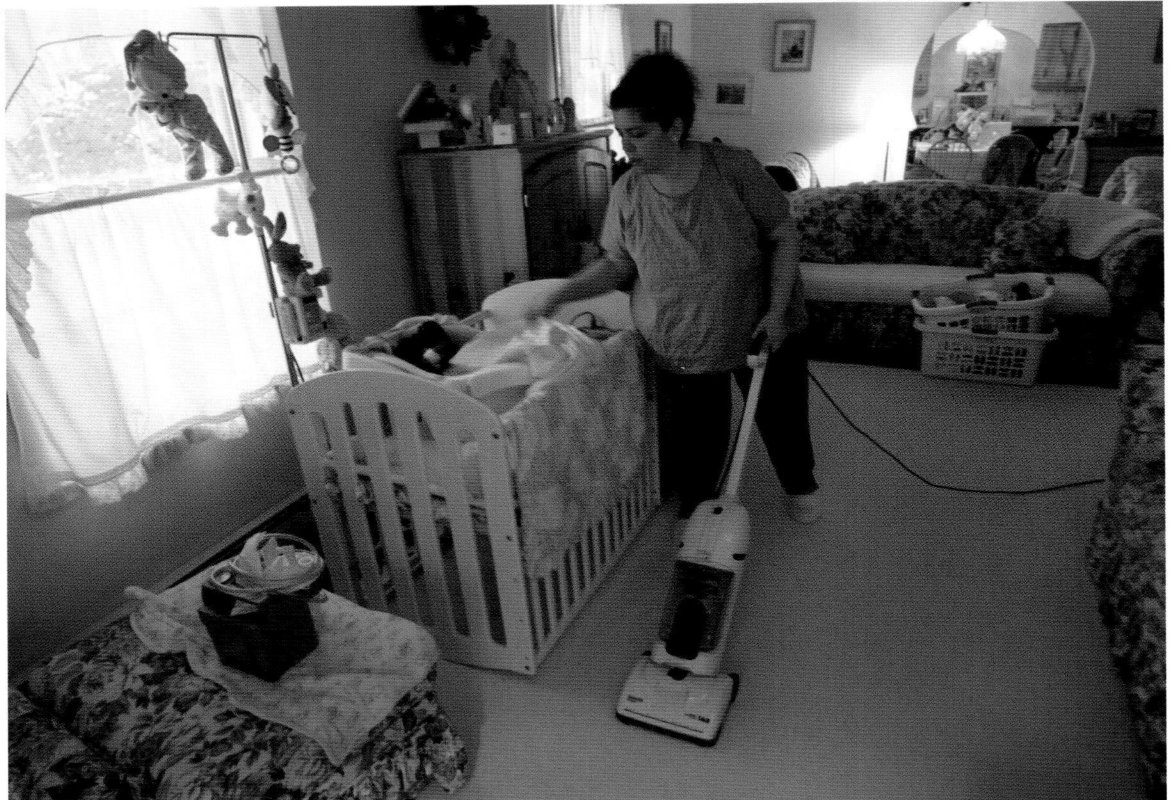

BEACHWOOD
Cindy and Ernie Davidson prepare dinner, while Zachariah investigates the refrigerator. The family shops for groceries four to five times a month and always looks for bulk items on sale.

BEACHWOOD
Davison, an equipment specialist at the Earle Naval Weapons Station, reads to Hannah, while Zachariah, 4, turns the pages. Zachariah, the Davisons' second adopted child, has Prader-Willi syndrome, a developmental and eating disorder. Davison says their care of the children is made possible by neighbors and church friends who have set up a response system to help them during emergencies.

MT. HOLLY

Twins Jackie Koch and Flo Jaquette not only look alike, but also live parallel lives. They both sang at USO canteens, taught junior high school, married and divorced, collected stuffed bears, dressed alike, and stayed within three miles of each other. Now that they're retired, the sisters have taken up singing show tunes at senior center events. "We're doing what we love," says Koch.

Photo by David M Warren

WALLINGTON

Think pink: Irene Barnas, aka The Pink Lady, has at least one doll and a splash of her favorite color in every corner of her house, from her living room, with its rose-colored drapes and couchside Raggedy Anne and Andy, to her pink-walled bedroom, decorated with Precious Moments–brand dolls. "Maybe I never grew up," she says. "I'm just an antique little girl."

Photo by Ellie Markovitch, The Herald News

ELIZABETH

When Susan Keogh's husband asked what she'd like to do for their 10th anniversary, she told him she wanted to have another child. Or five. Although the fertility treatments she'd taken during her first two pregnancies yielded one baby at each birth, she had always hoped for multiples. Voilà! On May 18, 2001, the Keogh quintuplets arrived.

Photos by Jason Towlen

ELIZABETH
"They're at that stage where they don't want their pictures taken, and then, if one starts crying, they all want to cry," says Keogh, 38, of her 2-year-old quintuplets Elizabeth, Brigid, Meaghan, Jacqueline, and Patrick.

ELIZABETH
While waiting for her husband to hang a clothesline, Keogh dries the quints' Mother's Day outfits on the swing set. Whenever she can find clothes in quintuplicate, Keogh dresses the children alike. "When I don't and I take them out, someone always comes up and says, 'Oh, how cute. What day care are you from?'"

HACKENSACK
Only 16 days old, Jessica Fonseca Colodeti is already an international citizen. Born to a Brazilian-Italian mother and a Costa Rican father, she is qualified for four passports. Mother Monica Colodeti plans to teach her daughter Portuguese, Italian, and Spanish. She says Jessica's first trip, to visit her grandmother in Brazil, is already in the works.
Photo by Mia Song, The Star-Ledger

WEST DEPTFORD
Michael and Diana Roche's daughter Theresa Marie was born with Spinal Muscular Dystrophy. The 2-year-old breathes through a ventilator and eats with a feeding tube. The family sought help in Lourdes and Rome. After meeting with Pope John Paul II, they prayed at the tomb of Pope John XXIII and asked for the "miracle of complete healing."
Photo by Gerald S. Williams

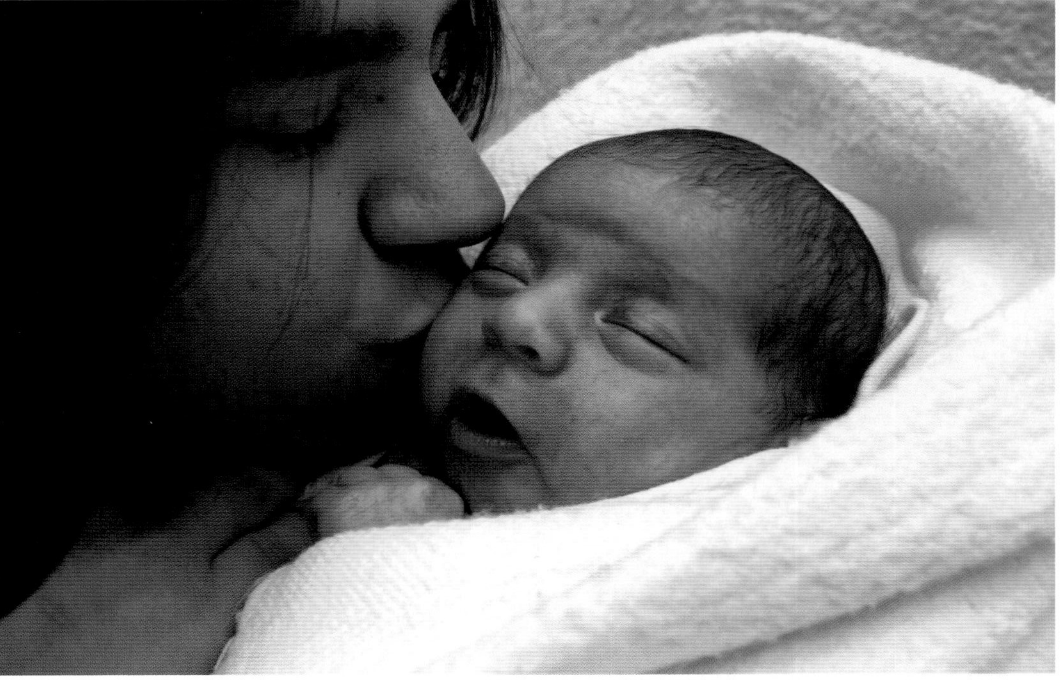

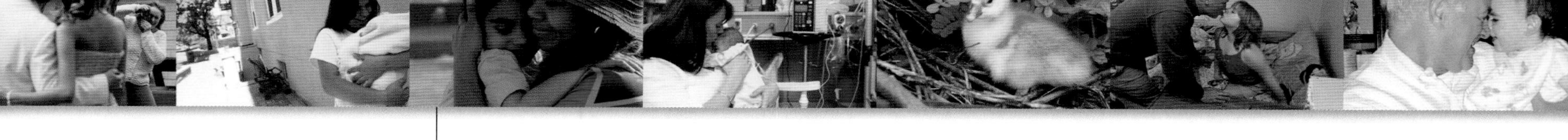

CAMDEN
Start 'em while they're young. A soccer league kicks off for children as young as five. Elizabeth Concepcion gives a little encouragement to her little girl Brianna, 6, at practice.
Photo by April Saul

LINDENWOLD

Partners since 1999, Ron Sproul and Ray Massaux solidified their commitment to each other in a ceremony at the Old First Reformed Church in Philadelphia in 2001. The two men love a good laugh. One of their preferred pastimes is watching game shows. Another is flipping through Ron's collection of 6,000 comic books. He says *Batman* and *Superman* are his favorites.

Photos by Sarah J. Glover, The Philadelphia Inquirer

CITY OF BURLINGTON

James Sanders, Austin Long, and Frederich Greene hold a coffee klatch, without the coffee. Every day they settle in on Sanders's front porch to comment on stories from *The Trentonian* and argue over how their favorite teams—the Philadelphia 76ers and the Philadelphia Eagles—are doing. And they might, on occasion, gossip about neighbors who pass by.

VINELAND
Ashley and Sandy Garrison race neighbor Tyler Simmerman down the only street in Victoria Mobile Home Park. Vineland has the largest concentration of mobile home parks in New Jersey. Many of the city's residents work in the surrounding fields or commute to casino jobs in nearby Atlantic City.
Photo by Danielle P. Richards

WEST CALDWELL
The predinner obstacle course: crawl over the couch, bounce on the pillow, then climb on the coffee table. Six-year-old Jacob Mulick and 3-year-old Ben give baby brother Sam, 17 months, a head start.
Photo by Daryl Stone, Asbury Park Press

HACKENSACK
Unofficial party photographer, Rhiannon Brown, 4, uses her disposable camera to grab a shot of 4-year-old birthday boy Sean Franklin at his Rescue Heroes–themed party.
Photo by Thomas E. Franklin

TABERNACLE

John Collins deadheads rhododendrons in his front yard. Since 1945, the gardener has single-handedly run his Spruce Farm Nursery, selling azaleas and rhododendrons out of his backyard and tending his private collection—including several 18-foot rhododendrons—in his front yard. "My wife tells me I can't buy any more flowers," he says. "I can only sell what I have."
Photo by Dennis McDonald, Burlington County Times

HUDSON COUNTY

With homeless shelters nearing capacity in Hudson County, some like Jacqueline build makeshift sheds under Hoboken's Conrail tracks or in the Palisade hills of nearby Union City. At one Hoboken food pantry, the number of families served each month has jumped from 60 in 1999 to 300 in 2003.

Photo by Shaul Schwarz, Corbis

he year 2003 marked a turning point in the history of photography: it was the first year that digital cameras outsold film cameras. To celebrate this unprecedented sea change, the *America 24/7* project invited amateur photographers—along with students and professionals—to shoot and, via the Internet, submit digital images. Think of it as audience participation. Their visions of community are interspersed with the professional frames throughout this book. On the following four pages, however, we present a gallery produced exclusively by amateur photographers.

RINGWOOD At the conclusion of the Revolutionary War on April 19, 1783, General Washington visited his mapmaker at Ringwood Manor, now a National Historic Landmark. ***Photo by Lisa Cogland***

OCEAN GROVE Founded as a Methodist retreat in 1869, Ocean Grove erects revival-style canvas tents every May to accommodate the 100-plus families who spend summers here. ***Photo by Paul Goldfinger***

CAPE MAY With more than 600 Victorian homes—many now converted into shops, inns, and restaurants—clustered at New Jersey's scenic southernmost tip, Cape May was declared a National Historic Landmark in 1976. ***Photo by Pam Brennan***

UNION George Diakides opened the Huck Finn Diner in 1994 just two miles from his uncle's Mark Twain Diner. Loyal locals keep both busy. ***Photo by Amanda Miller***

WEST CALDWELL When faced with a tough deadline, Bob Ross, director of digital imaging at The Corporate Communications Group, dons the Disaster Team hat to rally the troops. ***Photo by Mark Baran***

POTTERSVILLE If the bold, black lettering doesn't keep unwanted visitors from approaching, Rocket the corgi will. ***Photo by Chod Lang***

EAST RUTHERFORD A crowd checks the latest harness race results at Meadowlands Race Track, where the fastest mile in harness racing history was set by Jenna's Beach Boy (1:47.3) on June 22, 1996. ***Photo by Chad Sutton***

JERSEY CITY From Jersey City's Liberty State Park, Ellis Island and the Statue of Liberty are only a 10-minute ferry ride away. ***Photo by George Farrell***

POINT PLEASANT BEACH
As the *Leah* pushes east into the Atlantic, Billy Gallagher gets set to heave a net overboard for the first drag of the day.
Photo by Peter Ackerman, Asbury Park Press

Hard At Work

FAIRVIEW
At the Drama nightclub, Fernando Villalona sings from his album Mal Acostumbrado, nominated for a 2003 Grammy Award for Best Merengue Album. The popular and prolific Villalona has recorded one album a year for 20 years.
Photo by James W. Anness

FAIRVIEW
Trumpet players Julio Cesar Gil and Francisco Guerra, members of Fernando Villalona's banc warm up back stage before swinging a full ho at Drama nightclub. Like Villalona, the two cor from the Dominican Republic, where merengu music originated in the mid-1800s.
Photo by James W. Anness

CLIFTON
Natalia Marri is Italian and German, but ever since taking a belly dancing class in 1993, she's been hooked on the Middle Eastern art form. In 2002, she founded Genie in a Bottle, a six-person troupe that performs throughout New Jersey and New York. On weekends, she dances at Toros, a Turkish Mediterranean restaurant.
Photo by Ellie Markovitch, The Herald News

GRUNDEN
GRUNDEN

POINT PLEASANT BEACH
Whiting used to be the main fish caught by the *Leah*, a 71-foot commercial fishing trawler. Now it is a mix of butterfish, monkfish, squid, whiting, lobsters, and clams. Captain Denis Lovgren believes warmer ocean temperatures are behind the decline of cold-water fish, like whiting and cod.
Photos by Peter Ackerman, Asbury Park Press

POINT PLEASANT BEACH
Once the fish are on deck, Billy Gallagher and William Lovgren separate them by type into plastic baskets; each basket holds about 90 pounds. The value of the catch depends on the kind of fish. Those protected like this striped bass are thrown back.

POINT PLEASANT BEACH
After being separated, the fish are hosed and put on ice. Back at the dock, they will be boxed and shipped. Destinations include the Fulton Fish Market in New York City, warehouses in Philadelphia and Boston, and "cutting houses" that prepare filets for use in processed foods.

POINT PLEASANT BEACH
The *Leah* moves out at 4 a.m. and doesn't return until dinnertime. Each member of the crew—Denis Lovgren, his brother William, and Billy Gallagher—works a four-day week since just two of them go out each day. Gallagher squeezes in the maximum two hours of shut-eye allowed per shift, while his partner takes the watch.
Photos by Peter Ackerman, Asbury Park Press

POINT PLEASANT BEACH
The *Leah* usually heads to the Mud Hole, a bowl-shaped depression 15 miles offshore, where most New Jersey fishing boats congregate. In the winter, the fish often move to the Hudson Canyon 75 miles offshore. Since that voyage takes 20 hours round-trip, the crew spends three nights at sea and runs into fishermen from the Carolinas, New York, and Rhode Island.

SECAUCUS
In April of 1997, cable news network MSNBC left Manhattan and moved into a 180,000 sq. ft., refurbished warehouse at the edge of the Meadowlands. The facility has the largest column-free "On-Air" newsroom on the East Coast, which allows for dramatic camera work on such news-chat shows as "Morning Line," anchored by Alex Witt.
Photo by Mark Greenberg, WorldPictureNews

HIGHLAND PARK
It's 3 a.m. and the bars are closed. Do you know where your burgers and fries are? For many, it's the White Rose Restaurant, a night-light to hungry bar moths who show up in droves after the local haunts close.
Photo by Scott Lituchy, The Star-Ledger

UPPER SADDLE RIVER
Julian Zerbini, 8, is the youngest member of the Alain Zerbini touring circus. The only clown in the 20-performer show, Julian started his act at age 3. Now he has the confidence to pick people from the audience to come up and dance with him on stage. Julian speaks Italian, Spanish, and English and does all his own makeup.
Photo by Danielle P. Richards

Carhartt
Original equipment
for the American worker

WOODBURY
"Homer," the fiberglass G.I., rushes mailman John Prelas on Broad Street. Stationed in front of Polsky's Workwear, Homer has suffered his share of indignities: He's been defaced, had his gun stolen (and returned), and been caught in a lengthy lip lock with a local teenager.
Photo by David M Warren

NEWARK BAY

With a 9 mm Beretta strapped to his hip, U.S. Coast Guard Reservist James Totten prepares to board a container ship in Newark Bay, an industrial, port-clogged backwater of New York Harbor. The Coast Guard is responsible for the security of 200 commercial vessels every day—and 3,000,000 containers every year—that enter the harbor, America's third-busiest port.

Photos by James W. Anness

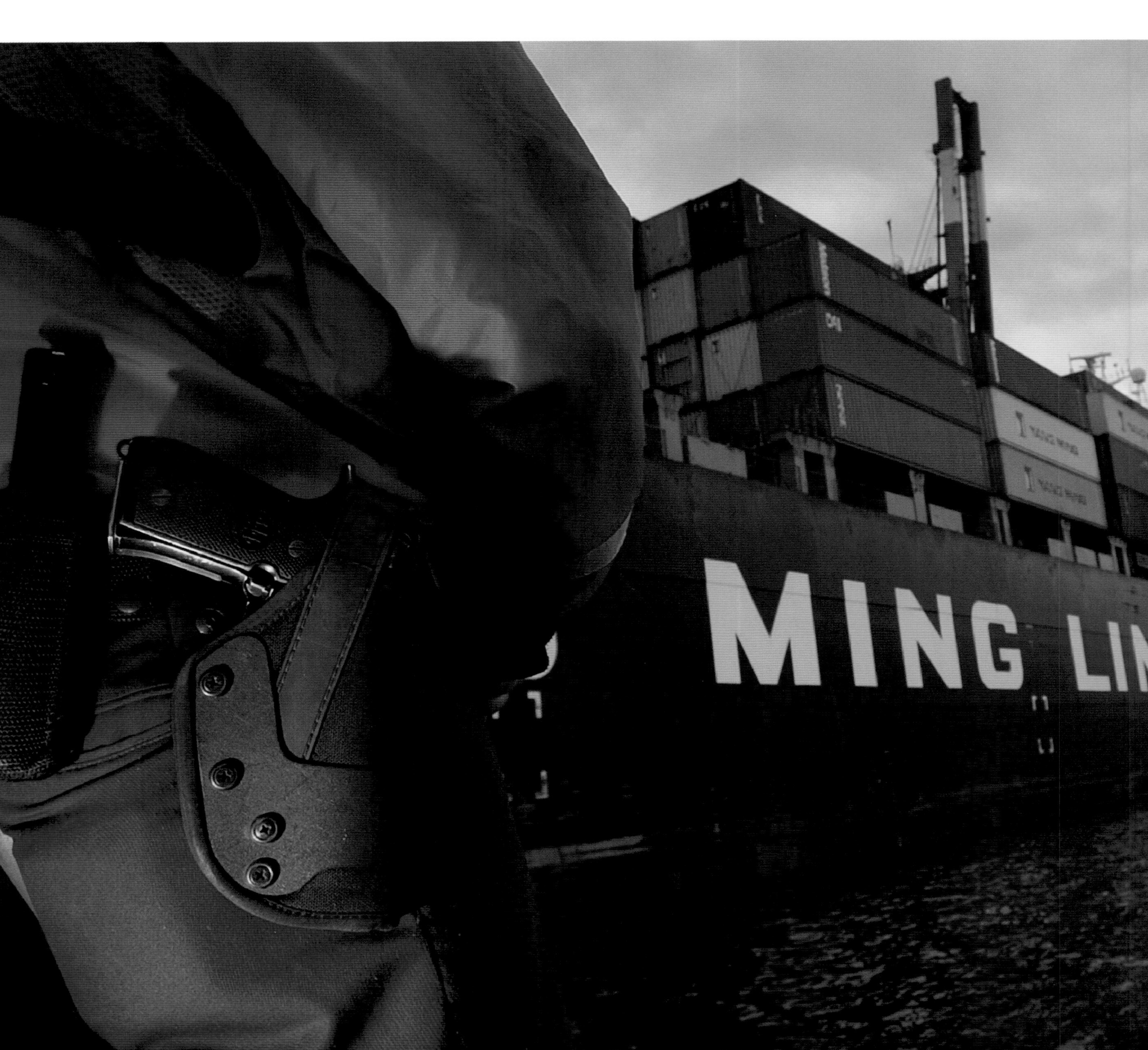

NEWARK BAY

Coxswain "Mac" MacDonald steers his 41-foot utility boat, while Reservist James Totten, a boarding team member, scans the horizon for a container ship that transmittted a distress call on its Eperb emergency system. It turns out the call was nothing but a switch that was flipped by mistake.

PORT ELIZABETH

In Port Elizabeth just off Kill Van Kull, a Coast Guard patrol boat approaches a container ship for a routine inspection. Since 9/11, MacDonald, one of the boat's reservist crew, has been activated twice for duty with the Coast Guard Station in Rosebank. Normally, he works as a police-man in the village of Quogue on Long Island.

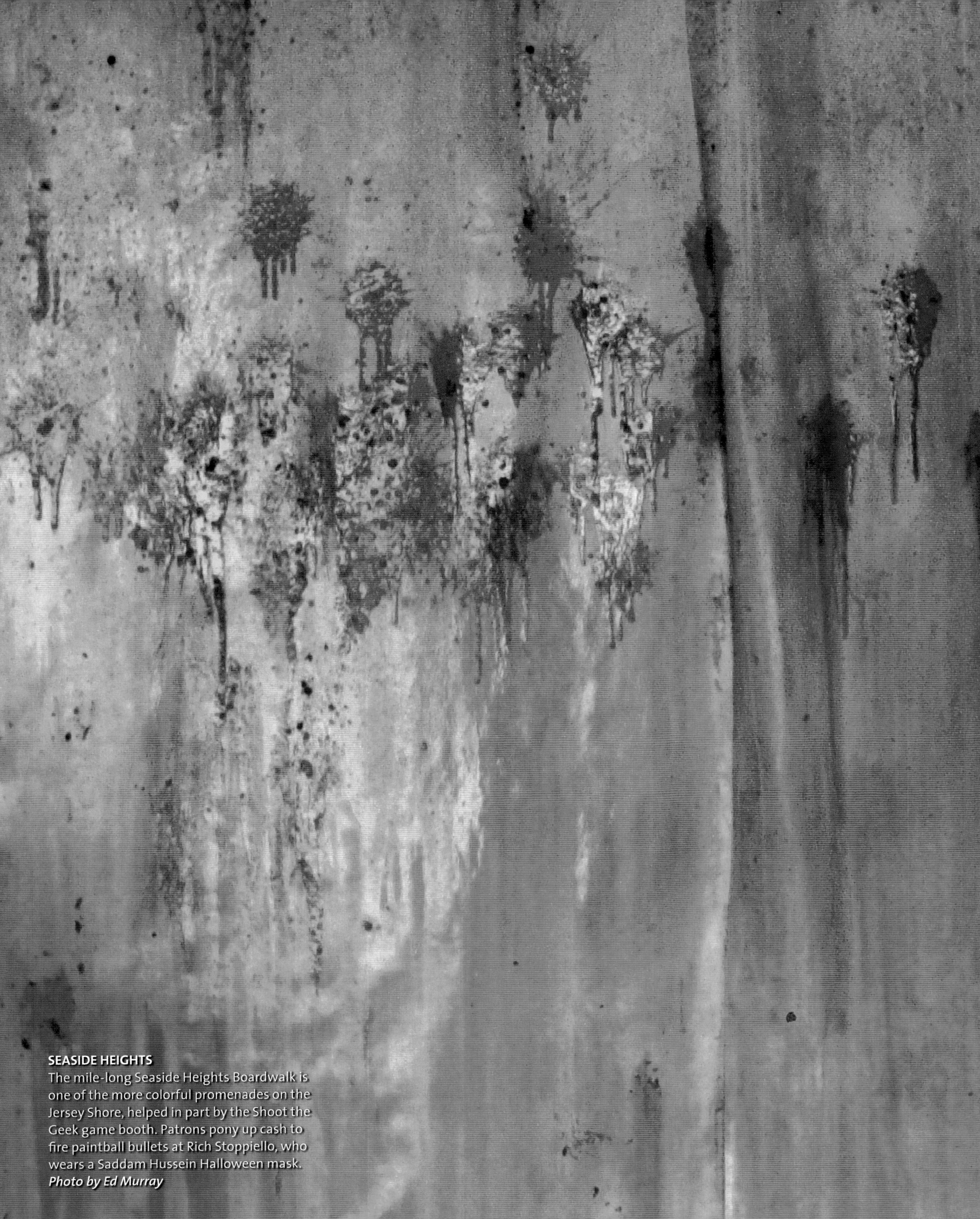

SEASIDE HEIGHTS
The mile-long Seaside Heights Boardwalk is one of the more colorful promenades on the Jersey Shore, helped in part by the Shoot the Geek game booth. Patrons pony up cash to fire paintball bullets at Rich Stoppiello, who wears a Saddam Hussein Halloween mask.
Photo by Ed Murray

CAMDEN

Started in 1993, Atlanta-based UniverSoul Circus is the first African-American-owned big top since the 1890s. Showgirl Mecca Johnson performs with African elephant Amy and Asian elephant Annamae. Is it true they have good memories? "Amazing," she says. "Sometimes they remind me to pick up my cue."

Photos by Aristide Economopoulos, The Star-Ledger

CAMDEN

Ameera Diamond is the only female African-American tiger trainer in the world. A former dancer with Ringling Bros. and Barnum & Bailey, she joined UniverSoul Circus where she learned to handle dogs, chimps, elephants—and finally 600-pound Siberian Tigers. "I have nine kids," she says. "Eight tigers and my son."

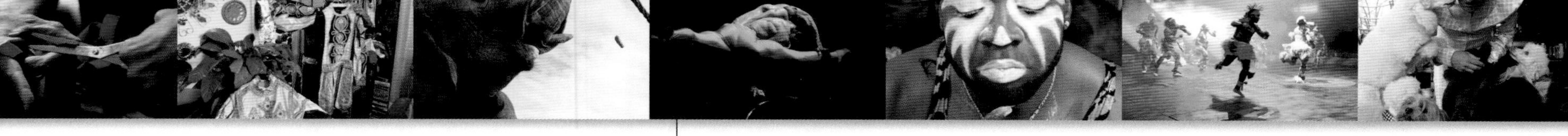

CAMDEN

After studying ballet in his native Cuba, acrobat Ricardo Sosa, 38, wanted a change and enrolled in a Russian circus school, where he learned hand balancing and contortion. That training, along with his natural athleticism, is the basis for the unique act he has performed worldwide with UniverSoul.

JERSEY CITY
When the PATH subway service to the World Trade Center in Manhattan was shut down after the attacks on 9/11, riders were diverted to the ferries. At Exchange Place's terminal, the number of daily commuters increased three-fold, from 1,600 to 4,800. Service on the PATH train was restored on November 23, 2003.
Photo by Thomas E. Franklin

MATAWAN
The commute, 7:25 a.m. Shawn Roalke, a writer for the National Hockey League website, rides a New Jersey Transit train to Penn Station and his job in midtown Manhattan. Matawan residents spend an average of an hour and 20 minutes commuting to work.
Photo by Daryl Stone, Asbury Park Press

NEWARK
After a day in the Manhattan salt mines, about 4,800 commuters arrive at Newark Penn Station. From here, they spread out across the state—New Jersey Transit's Raritan Valley line covers West Jersey, the Northeast Corridor line makes its way southwest to Trenton, and the North Jersey Coast line serves the Atlantic coast as far south as Bay Head.
Photo by Ed Murray

BERGENFIELD
A landscaper needs one man for a day's work but dozens line up to earn the $10.00 hourly wage. He who moves the fastest and speaks a little English usually gets the job. On average, 60 day laborers look for work every morning at a corner in Bergenfield called "the base."
Photos by James W. Anness

BERGENFIELD
Every morning between 6 a.m. and noon, William Archbold, a Unification Church missionary, goes to a day laborers' pick-up spot to teach basic English classes. The biligual Archbold says, "They learn practical things like 'How much do you pay?'"

BERGENFIELD
A group of *los jornaleros*, or day laborers, flock around a roofing contractor as he hires a day crew. Most of the men come from Mexico, Guatemala, El Salvador, and Peru, and more than 80 percent are undocumented immigrants.

JACKSON
In the African wild, a 15-foot tall, reticulated giraffe forages for food an average of 15 to 20 hours a day. At the Six Flags Wild Safari, life is a little easier. Four of the park's 12 giraffes eat an alfalfa snack from supervisor Doreen Garruto's truck. Reticulated refers to the animal's distinctive markings.
Photo by Daryl Stone, Asbury Park Press

ATLANTIC CITY

Viva Atlantic City: Backstage at "Legends In Concert," Elvis impersonator James Lowrey tackles an NFL video game in his dressing room. He's performed as the King for 14 years, the past three at the Claridge Casino at Bally's. The performing bug bit in second grade when Lowrey first sang "Love Me Tender."

Photos by April Saul

ATLANTIC CITY
It's a fast-paced life that Linda Suarez (left) and Kristen Hendrick lead as "Legends In Concert" back-up singers and dancers. There are ten costume changes in every show, some as quick as 30 seconds. They even do back-up singing sometimes while changing. "It's hard to hold a note when you're bending down hooking things," says Suarez.

ATLANTIC CITY
Dancer Maria Washington does two shows a night, six nights a week, backing up an ever-changing group of superstar impersonators ranging from Elvis, Cher, and Tony Bennett to Michael Jackson and Bette Midler.

HOBOKEN

Ireno Rodriquez's Antique Bakery relies on daily coal deliveries to produce its renowned Hoboken bread. Baked over the coals for five hours, the bread has a pungent flavor and crisp crust. One of only three bakeries left in the area that bake these Italian-style baguettes, Antique Bakery sells more than 1,000 loaves a day.
Photo by Thomas E. Franklin

JERSEY CITY
At El Saraya Coffee Shop, a Middle Eastern grill and juice bar, Chef Sanem George twirls a piece of paper-thin, tire-size dough in the air before slapping it down on the counter to make *fetir*, the Egyptian version of pizza. The dough is filled with sweet or savory ingredients and folded into a rectangle that's cooked in a pizza oven.
Photo by Aristide Economopoulos, The Star-Ledger

ATLANTIC CITY
"I'm not going to let any grass grow under my feet!" says Anna Cucco, 84. A member of five different social clubs, Cucco joins the 3 H (Health, Hope and Happiness) Club on its regular trips to Atlantic City. An hour bus ride from Clementon delivers the group to a buffet dinner and show, and then it's off to the slots.
Photo by Akira Suwa, The Philadelphia Inquirer

New Jersey At Play
PLAY
3
CREDITS

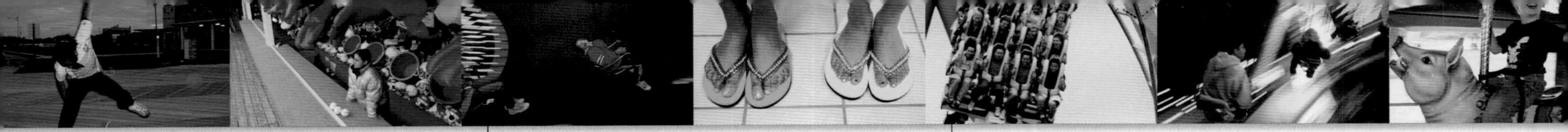

WILDWOOD

The Morey the merrier: A Girl Scout rides the Waveswinger at Morey's Piers. She's one of 9,000 Girl Scouts and Boy Scouts in town for the Ninth Annual Beach Jam. The Scouts and their leaders, who come from eight states and Ontario, Canada, camp out on the beach in front of the three amusement piers.

Photo by Scott Lituchy, The Star-Ledger

JACKSON TOWNSHIP

It loops, spirals, and corkscrews, traveling at speeds up to 61 mph along 3,985 feet of track. Six Flags Great Adventure's Medusa is the first floorless roller coaster. Passengers dangle their feet over the rails—but there's no slot for an airsickness bag.

Photo by Noah K. Murray

TEANECK
Girls at the coed 220-student Muslim junior-senior high school, Al-Ghazaly, jump rope during lunch break. Muslim religious and cultural beliefs prohibit girls from appearing in public without their *hijab*, or headcover.
Photo by Danielle P. Richards

JERSEY CITY
Ibrahim Atalla puffs on sweetened tobacco through a *nagile* (hookah) at the El Saraya Coffee Shop, a popular Egyptian hangout in Jersey City. According to the Arab American Institute, New Jersey's Arab-speaking population is the fastest growing of any state in the nation.
Photo by Aristide Economopoulos, The Star-Ledger

OXFORD
Captain Bill Strunk from Stroudsburg, Pennsylvania, takes a break from the stress of the Revolutionary War at the annual Warren County Heritage Festival. A member of Craig's Artillery, Strunk reenacts many skirmishes. Almost 100 Revolutionary War battles were fought in New Jersey, which became known as "the cockpit of the revolution."
Photo by Ed Murray

WOOD-RIDGE
Something to talk about: Hudson Catholic High School senior Patrick Sidhom cools down while his date, Sophia Rodriguez, checks in. The high school held its 2003 prom "Heaven" at the Fiesta Banquet Rooms, overseen—in oil at least—by Fiesta's founder, Rose Landry.
Photo by Aristide Economopoulos, The Star-Ledger

NEPTUNE
Amber Ciez, 18, and Kyle Knichel, 17, slow dance to Kelly Clarkson's "A Moment Like This" during the Keyport High School Prom at Jumping Brook Country Club on the Jersey shore. The predominately white public school enrolls about 590 students.
Photo by Daryl Stone, Asbury Park Press

WOOD-RIDGE
Ki-Ameer Silk Johnson and his date at the Fiesta Banquet Hall for the Hudson Catholic High School prom. The Christian Brothers boys school located in Jersey City has a student body that reflects the diversity of the area—530 students from 54 different countries who speak 37 different languages.
Photo by Aristide Economopoulos, The Star-Ledger

P S F
ARAMARK
0

CAMDEN
In a parking lot, a game of round ball heats up between drumline member Terry Thomas and Gabonese acrobats Cedric Abyi, Jean Thomas Madoundou, and Jim Moussauou—all of them performers with the touring, Atlanta-based UniverSoul Circus. Looming in the background, across the Delaware River, is Philadelphia.
Photo by Aristide Economopoulos, The Star-Ledger

BEDMINSTER
Trout and about: A fisherman with his take from the North Branch of the Raritan River, stocked each year with 17,000 trout.
Photos by Ed Murray

ISLAND BEACH
John Lenart of Roosevelt comes to Island Beach State Park every weekend to surf fish for striped bass and croakers. A special permit allows him to drive his four-wheel-drive truck right onto the big beach. And if he's not with his two boys, he camps overnight. "You can fish from midnight to 4 a.m. if you want," says the angler.

LEBANON TOWNSHIP
The South Branch of the Raritan River rushes through the Ken Lockwood Gorge, where Chris Opdyke and James Hrubesh set up to do some fly fishing, hoping to snag some trout.

RINGWOOD
To accommodate the growing water needs of Passaic County, the Monksville Reservoir was built in the late 1980s. It flooded the former town of Monksville whose fields are now filled with muskellunge, walleye, and bass.
Photo by Danielle P. Richards

Fleet
LAND ROVER
PRINCETON
Drivers wanted.
We're #1 with Patriots coverage.
UNITED TRUST
MADISON JAGUA
You can do it. We can help.
UNEEDA
10
24

BRIDGEWATER
Somerset Patriots outfielder Marcus Knight prepares to bat against the Long Island Ducks at Commerce Bank Ballpark. The Atlantic League of Professional Baseball Clubs is not affiliated with the major or minor leagues. Several of the league's eight teams are managed by former pros like Sparky Lyle and Butch Hobson
Photo by Ed Murray

RAHWAY

Dan Wargo, Leo Murcia, and Nick Veltre are three-fourths of A Match Like Memory. Twice a month, the teens can be heard in local clubs working out their sound. It's punk but not really punk. "We're more like Taking Back Sunday than The Ramones," says drummer Joe Geis.

Photos by Scott Lituchy, The Star-Ledger

GLEN RIDGE
Saturday Night Fever, the early years: Dressed in her grandmother's poncho, 7-year-old Niav O'Connor (center) dances the night away at the parent-student Disco Night sponsored by Linden Avenue School. The kids boogied to the beat of the Bee Gees and Donna Summer.

ASBURY PARK
A young family follows the Sunday service at Cathedral Assembly by the Shore, a 101-year-old Pentecostal Baptist church with 7,000 members and locations in Perth Amboy and Plainfield. The assembly has its own halfway house, day care center, grade school, and café, and has built affordable housing for its members.
Photo by Daryl Stone, Asbury Park Press

Reason To Believe

UPPER SADDLE RIVER
Susan Tudisco holds 6-month-old daughter Katherine as she and her mother Lori Geiger sing with the choir at the Old Stone Church. Started in 1784, it is part of the Reformed Church in America, a denomination that traces its roots to the Dutch who settled Manhattan.
Photos by Mark Greenberg, WorldPictureNews

UPPER SADDLE RIVER
William and Lori Schmid watch Reverend Robert Fretz, minister of the Old Stone Church, baptize daughter Juliana. They're part of the church's 180-member congregation. "Bergen County has over 500 small Protestant churches," says Fretz. "There are no megachurches here. People feel overwhelmed by mega-everything and want something personal."

UPPER SADDLE RIVER
Reverend Fretz preaches from an antique pulpit in the restored Old Stone Church, built in 1819. The second-story balcony, which is now the choir loft, was originally set aside for servants and slaves—some of whom carved their initials in the narrow, ten-inch wide seats.

IN LOVING MEMO
OF THOSE LOST F
HOBOKEN ON 9/1

JOAO "JJ" A.F. AG
JEAN ANN ANDRU
PETER PAUL APOL
DONNA BERNAER
MARTIN BORYCZE

HOBOKEN
To honor the people of Hoboken who lost their lives on 9/11, the city erected this memorial in Pier A Park, across the Hudson River from Manhattan. Each plexiglass panel lists 14 names, honoring a total of 56 people who died. Ginkgo Biloba trees (one of the few tree species to survive the Hiroshima blast) were planted nearby as a living tribute.
Photo by Scott Lituchy, The Star-Ledger

CLIFTON
During burial services in East Ridgelawn Cemetery, Isidra Bastardo grieves inconsolably at the grave of her sister Feliciana Santana. The two sisters grew up in Puerto Rico, and when Feliciana came to New Jersey 12 years ago, they kept in touch with weekly phone calls. Now the family honor her life with a mass each month and Sunday visits to her grave.
Photo by Daryl Stone, Asbury Park Press

CAMDEN
Renita Singleton joins members of the Vessels for Christ dance ministry at Parkside United Methodist Church. The group is performing at Praise Fest, an annual gathering of praise-dance groups. Vessels for Christ, created in 1998, is part of a movement in Christianity to include liturgical dance in worship services.
Photo by Sarah J. Glover, The Philadelphia Inquirer

MONMOUTH JUNCTION
Founded in 1973 as an outgrowth of a Rutgers University student organization, the Islamic Society of Central Jersey now has more than 2,000 member families. Every Friday afternoon, they gather for Jum'aa, the communal bow toward Mecca.
Photo by Jason Towlen

CAMDEN
Former social worker Marianne Holler decided to enter medical school—at age 40. She graduated four years later, and asked friend Monsignor Michael Doyle of Sacred Heart Church to anoint her hands. The "healing hands" ceremony at the chapel of Our Lady of Lourdes Hospital was in lieu of a party. "I'm too old for streamers," she says.
Photo by April Saul

WEST LONG BRANCH
An electric stair glider helps Brady Dupre reach the apartment she shares with her mother. Brady, 13, has ectrodactylism—a genetic disorder characterized by missing fingers and toes. Brady was also born without a tibia in either leg, so both her legs were amputated just above the knee before she turned 2.
Photos by Peter Ackerman, Asbury Park Press

WEST LONG BRANCH
During lunch break, Brady (center), Mackenzie Flannigan, and Erin Piner scan pictures taken at a school dance. At one dance, seventh-grader Brady and a friend dressed in glitter outfits and performed Abba's "Dancing Queen" for the lip-synch contest.

WEST LONG BRANCH

Despite her enthusiasm for school—she is president of the Spanish club, a member of the yearbook committee, and counsels younger kids as part of the Peer Leadership program—some mornings can be tough for Brady. Dependent on artificial legs, she has to get a new set every year to keep up with her growth.

Photos by Peter Ackerman, Asbury Park Press

FORT MONMOUTH
Brady's dad is a retired Army officer, which entitles her to privileges at Fort Monmouth. Her favorite perk is the pool. She removes her prosthetic legs in the locker room, crawls to the edge, and jumps in. Even with her malformed hands, she is able to pull herself out of the water when she is done.

WEST LONG BRANCH
Brady at bat in gym class (friends run the bases for her). She has been a baton twirler with the band and played baseball with the local league for the handicapped. Her mom Maureen supports her efforts. "I let her try everything. Otherwise, she won't know what she can do."

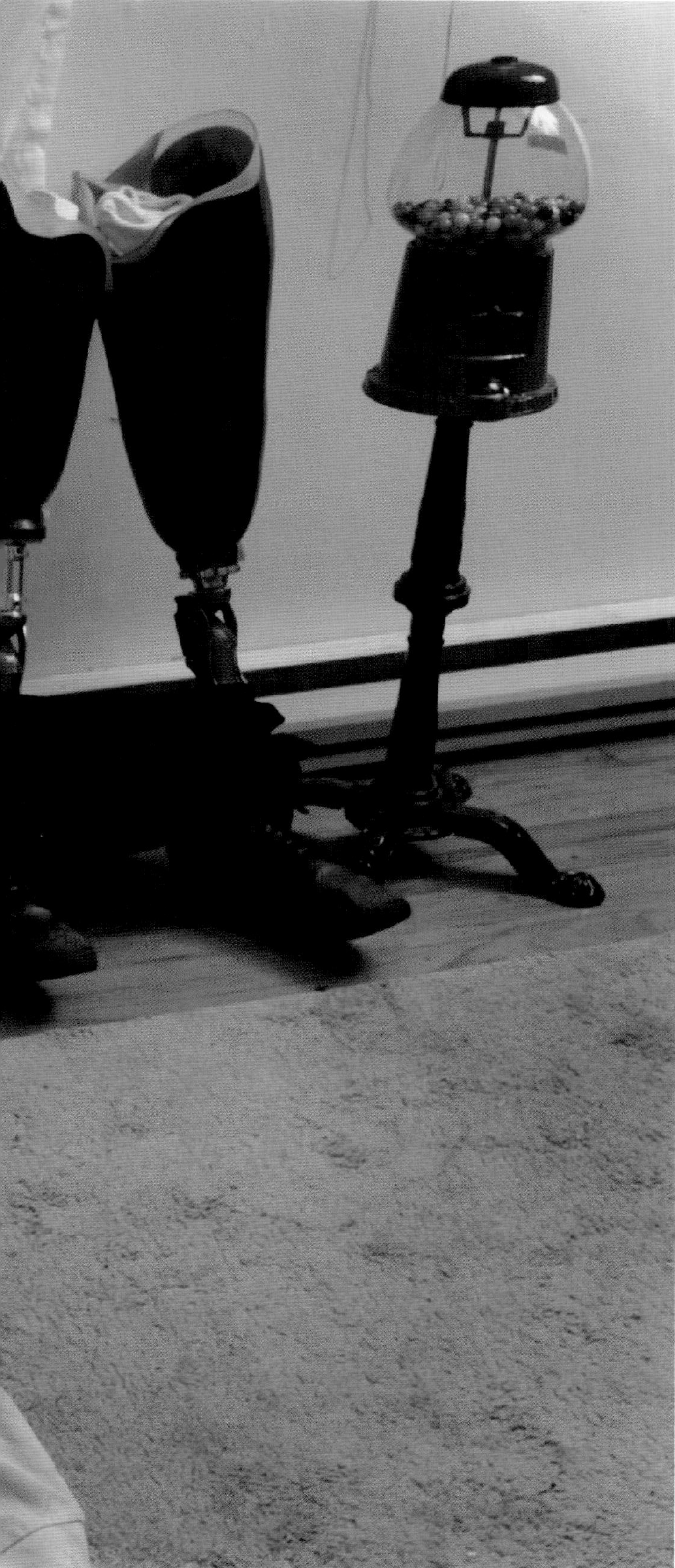

ABERDEEN
Nate Chadwick, owner of Fat Kat Tattoo, puts finishing touches on "The Serenity Prayer" which Doug Dobson, 26, wears to show his commitment to the Narcotics Anonymous 12-step program. Dobson, who has been clean for three years, went without a shirt most of the summer. He says, "The tattoo gets lots of comments."
Photos by Daryl Stone, Asbury Park Press

ASBURY PARK

With Pentecostal fervor, worshippers stand and pray during Sunday morning services at the Cathedral Assembly by the Shore, a Baptist church organized by 35 African Americans in 1892. During the past 20 years, under the guidance of senior pastor Bishop Donald Hilliard, Jr. church membership has tripled.

SANDY HOOK
Home to the Fort Hancock naval base until its closure in 1974, the six-and-a-half mile peninsula of Sandy Hook, which juts dramatically into the approach to New York Harbor, is best known today for its hiking trails and beaches. The 200-year-old quarters on Officer's Row are a reminder of the strategic site's past.
Photo by Brian Smiga, Preclick

Our Town

WILDWOOD

The boardwalk at Wildwood is one of the biggest, brightest, and loudest along the Jersey shore. But at this particular moment, Nina Hacker, 16, and boyfriend Mike Pericoloso, 18, don't seem to notice...or care.

Photo by Scott Lituchy, The Star-Ledger

HAMILTON SQUARE
Ryan Mapes, 18, splurged for the Steinert High School prom with professional make-up, an upswept hairdo with pink flowers to match her dress, and a French manicure and pedicure. Despite all the glamour, it was raining that night, so she threw a pair of tennis shoes on to dash to the limousine, and ended up wearing them all night.
Photo by Barry Fellman

WILDWOOD
Hold the onions: Corinne Boyle, 19, and boyfriend Vic McHugh, 21, engage in a little full-frontal snogging near a pizza shop on the boardwalk.
Photo by Scott Lituchy, The Star-Ledger

LONG BEACH ISLAND

After a winter's worth of storms, homeowners in the beach town of Loveladies on Long Beach Island shored up their shrinking front yards with bulldozers. In 1962, a brutal nor'easter wiped out most of the houses in Loveladies, one of a string of upscale summer colonies on Long Beach Island.

Photos by Dennis McDonald, Burlington County Times

BERKELEY

Unlike most suburban developments, which grew around company towns as commuter communities, these Midway Beach bungalows were built strictly for summer fun—open floor plans with no insulation or heating. Developed between 1920 and 1960, the 500-square-foot bungalows originally sold for $2,500 and now go for more than $200,000.

ATLANTIC CITY
A pier juts out from the Boardwalk and gives perches to sea-gazers and sun worshippers. City planners thought locals would fish from the ends of the minipiers at high tide. Turns out local surf fishermen prefer casting from the beach or nearby sea walls.
Photos by Nicola A. Menzie

ATLANTIC CITY

The Monopoly gameboard lifted its street names straight out of Atlantic City. The streets have also inspired iconic art installations along the Boardwalk, like this cored apple at New York Avenue. Other fancies along the Boardwalk include pink flamingos at Florida Avenue and a director's chair and movie camera at California Avenue.

FORT LEE
High above the Hudson River, painters apply 35,000 gallons of gray paint to the 73-year-old George Washington Bridge, one of the busiest in the country. The three-year, $54 million project is part of a post–9/11, $9.5 billion investment in metropolitan New York's transportation systems.
Photo by James W. Anness

TABERNACLE

Talif Mitchell, Jorge Ramirez, Peter Near, Jr., and Qiydaar Patterson respond to commands befo barracks clean-up and inspection at New Jerse Wharton Forest boot camp. Modeled after the military—correctional officers are drill instructors; participants are cadets—the six-month program is an alternative to incarceration for teenagers convicted of nonviolent crimes.
Photos by Peter Ackerman, Asbury Park Press

TABERNACLE
Jorge Ramirez, second in line, spent three months in a correctional facility before being sent to boot camp. He says he's learning patience and respect for others. "It's hard to keep your cool when a drill instructor is screaming in your face, but you learn it's for your own good."

TABERNACLE
Boot camp demands that teenage cadets do classwork, chores, counseling sessions, and community service. It also imposes a physical regimen with an eight-set Marine Corps bodybuilder routine. Cadet Qiydaar Patterson does the first set, combining push-ups, claps, and mule kicks.

CLIFTON

As any goombah will tell you, there's lots of waiting around on the set. HBO's *The Sopranos* is no exception. Prior to shooting a scene at the Upper Montclair Country Club, costumer Elizabeth Feldbauer delints Emmy winner James Gandolfini's shirt. Gandolfini, better known as antihero Tony Soprano, shares a cart with Robert Funaro, who plays Eugene Pontecorvo.

Photos by April Saul

HADDONFIELD
Kirk Heist, Timmy Vitez, Mark Goodwin, and J.J. Stanton all vie for the title "Mr. Haddonfield Memorial High School." The faux beauty pageant showcased a dozen seniors performing tongue-in-chic autobiographical skits and musical numbers, mostly in drag. Sadly, the fire alarm was pulled before a winner could be crowned.

HOBOKEN
A Manhattanite's bachelorette party runs into a serious clubbing crowd at the River Street Experience. Since March 30, 2003, when New York City banned smoking in all bars and restaurants, business has picked up in Hoboken. Four different nightclubs, easily accessible by bus, ferry, train, and car from Manhattan, cluster near the Hudson River waterfront.
Photo by Shaul Schwarz, Corbis

SEASIDE HEIGHTS
Shore stud: Twenty-something Cody-something from Philadelphia struts his stuff along the boardwalk at Seaside Heights. In addition to freely offered stares, the young man says, older women often come over and ask to buy him a drink.
Photo by Ed Murray

Charles Manson
a.k.a. Jesus Christ
oi!

CLINTON
The United Methodist Church, as seen from Dead Man's Curve on Route 31 in Clinton, pop. 2,632. The picturesque town, 45 miles west of New York City, is known for its historic Red Mill, frequent Civil War reenactments, and Victorian Dickens Weekends.
Photos by Ed Murray

CLINTON
Canoes from Clinton Canoe and Kayak await rental on the South Branch of the Raritan River. The headwaters of the South Branch flow out of Budd Lake. Passing through towns it has nourished for centuries—Long Valley, Califon, Washington Township, Chester—the river eventually empties into Raritan Bay just south of Staten Island at Perth Amboy.

THE MEADOWLANDS
Before 1968, Jerseyans used the Meadowlands, an 18,000-acre marsh stretching 15 miles from Hackensack to Harrison, as a dumping ground. That all changed when the Meadowlands Commission, a state agency, began to clean up and protect the unique estuarine ecosystem, three miles from Manhattan.
Photo by Ed Murray

SEA BRIGHT
Beneath the scenic surface, a battle rages between sea and sand. To bulk up the beach, the federal government pumped the equivalent of a half million truckloads of sand from the ocean floor onto the Sea Bright public beach in 1995. Scientists attribute much of the erosion along the state's 127 miles of Atlantic coastline to rising sea levels caused by global warming.
Photo by Brian Smiga, Preclick

PINE BARRENS
In the nation's most densely populated state, the one-million-acre Pinelands National Reserve encompasses seven counties and 52 municipalities. Under the rules establishing the Reserve, private land owners, such as the deed holder to this stand of Atlantic White Cedars, may petition the state for logging permits.
Photo by Dennis McDonald, Burlington County Times

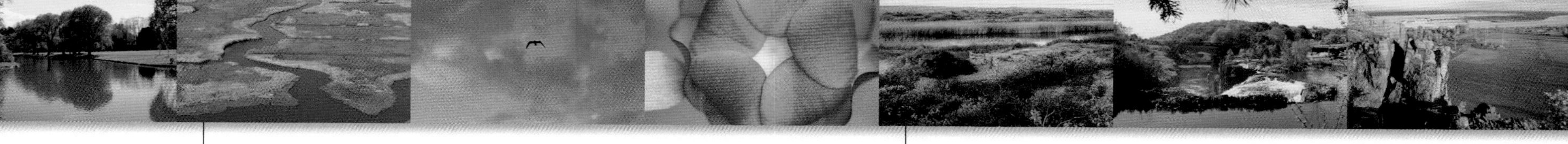

MULLICA RIVER
Named for a Swedish pioneer, the Mullica River rises near Camden and flows 55 miles southeast through the Pinelands before broadening into wetlands at the Great Bay.
Photo by Dennis McDonald, Burlington County Times

SANDY HOOK
At the north end of Sandy Hook, Fisherman's Trail winds through beach plum, sumac, and seaside golden rod on its way to the ocean.
Photo by Brian Smiga, Preclick

JERSEY CITY
Across the Hudson, fog fills the space that once belonged to the World Trade Center.
Photo by Thomas E. Franklin

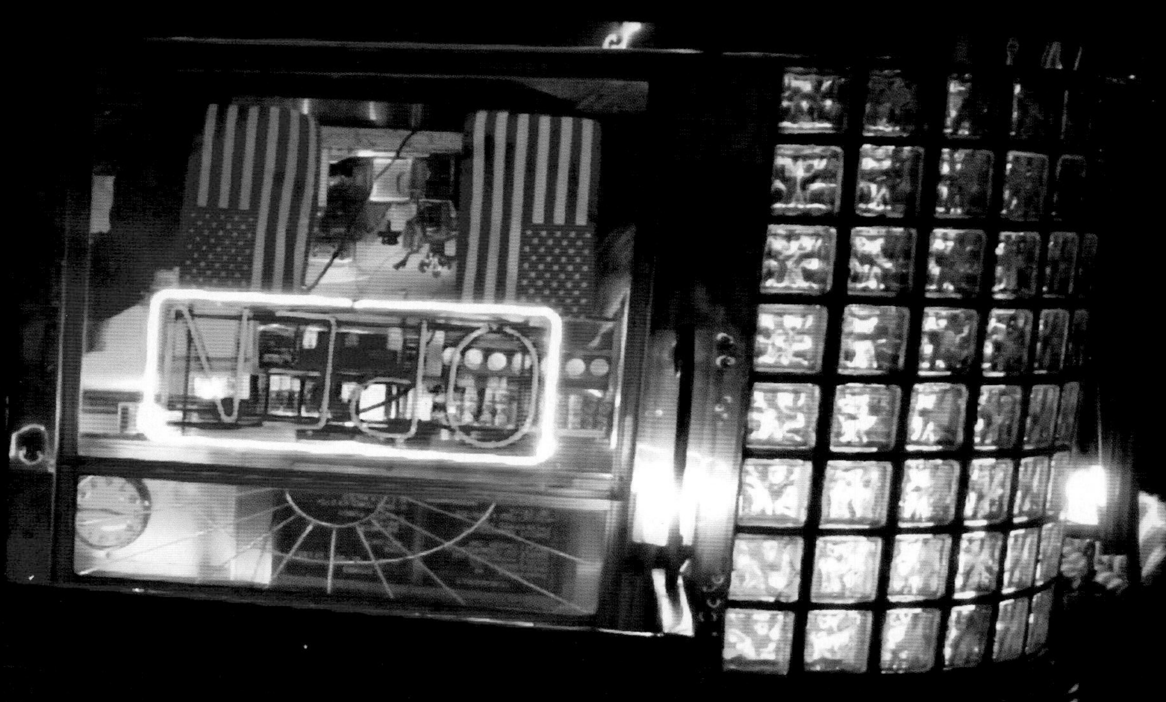

HACKENSACK
For more than 60 years, White Manna has been a landmark on River Road. The old-time Jersey diner is reliable for its "sliders," neat little hamburgers served with a side of pickles or fries for less than $3.
Photo by Thomas E. Franklin

The week of May 12-18, 2003, more than 25,000 professional and amateur photographers spread out across the nation to shoot over a million digital photographs with the goal of capturing the essence of daily life in America.

The professional photographers were equipped with Adobe Photoshop and Adobe Album software, Olympus C-5050 digital cameras, and Lexar Media's high-speed compact flash cards.

The 1,000 professional contract photographers plus another 5,000 stringers and students sent their images via FTP (file transfer protocol) directly to the *America 24/7* website. Meanwhile, thousands of amateur photographers uploaded their images to Snapfish's servers.

At *America 24/7*'s Mission Control headquarters, located at CNET in San Francisco, dozens of picture editors from the nation's most prestigious publications culled the images down to 25,000 of the very best, using Photo Mechanic by Camera Bits. These photos were transferred into Webware's ActiveMedia Digital Asset Management (DAM) system, which served as a central image library and enabled the designers to track, search, distribute, and reformat the images for the creation of the 51 books, foreign language editions, web and magazine syndication, posters, and exhibitions.

Once in the DAM, images were optimized (and in some cases resampled to increase image resolution) using Adobe Photoshop. Adobe InDesign and Adobe InCopy were used to design and produce the 51 books, which were edited and reviewed in multiple locations around the world in the form of Adobe Acrobat PDFs. Epson Stylus printers were used for photo proofing and to produce large-format images for exhibitions. The companies providing support for the *America 24/7* project offer many of the essential components for anyone building a digital darkroom. We encourage you to read more on the following pages about their respective roles in making *America 24/7* possible.

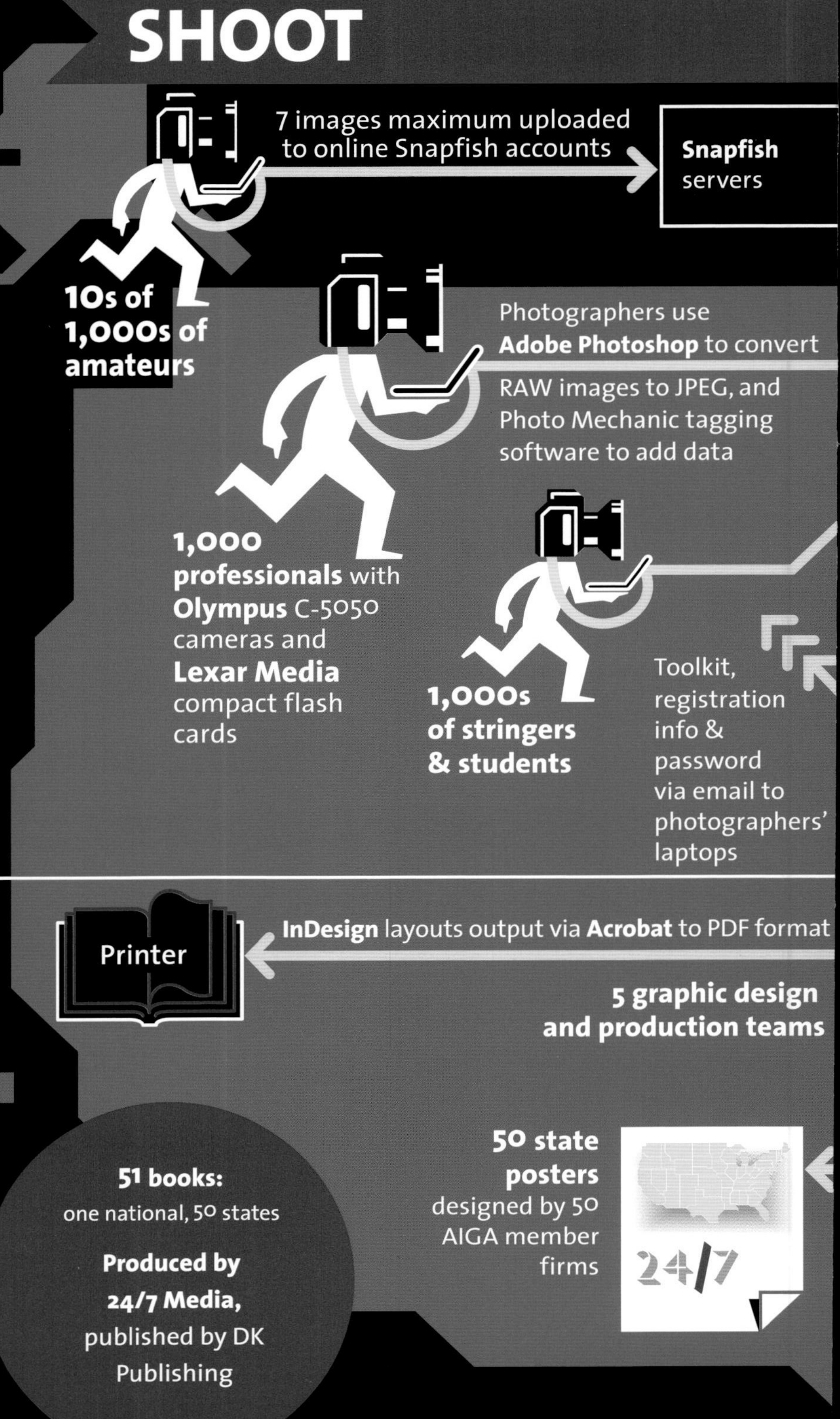

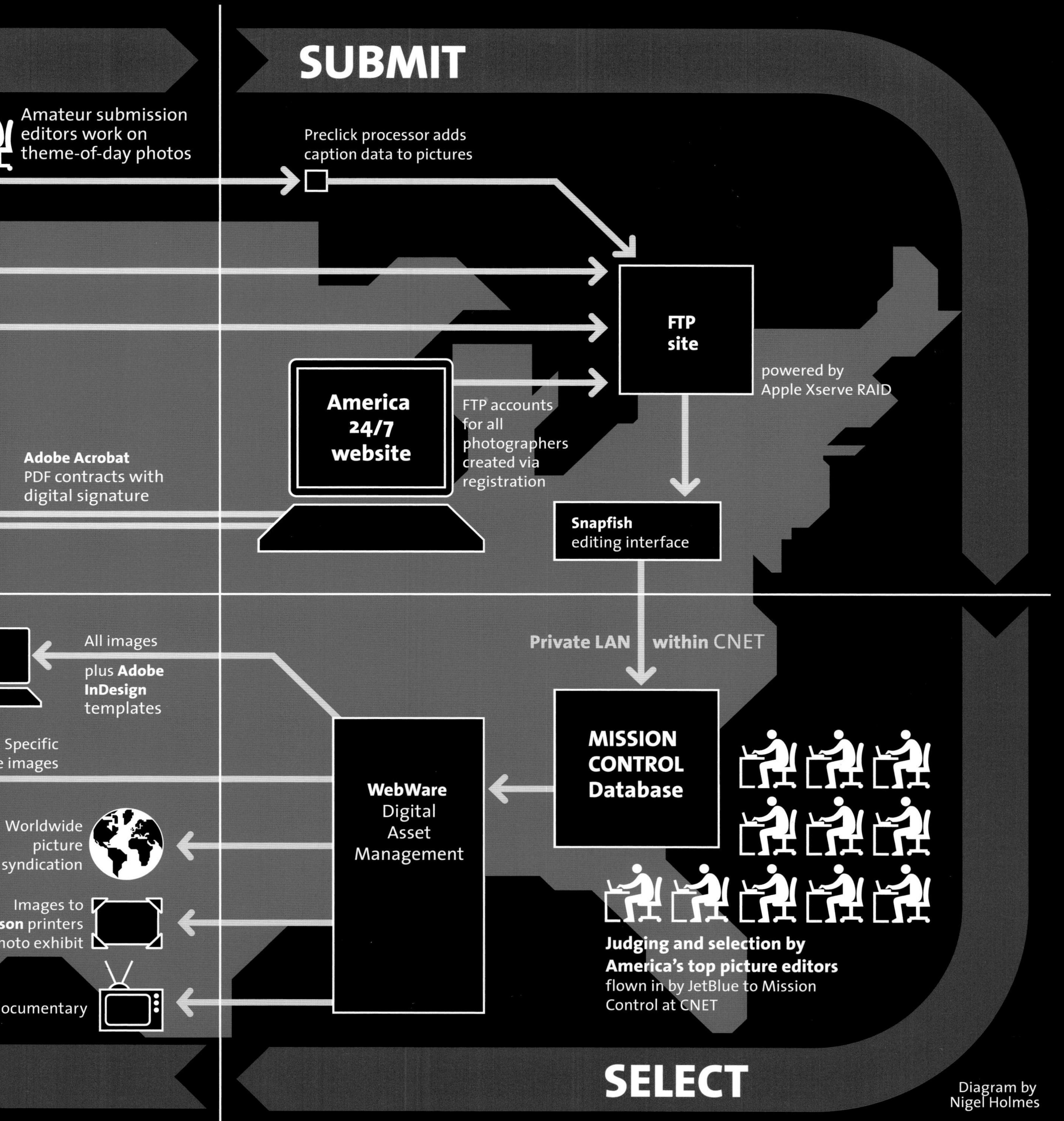

Diagram by Nigel Holmes

About Our Sponsors

Adobe

America 24/7 gave digital photographers of all levels the opportunity to share their visions of what it means to live in the United States. This project was made possible by a digital photography revolution that is dramatically changing and improving picture-taking for professionals and amateurs alike. And an Adobe product, Photoshop®, has been at the center of this sea change.

Adobe's products reflect our customers' passion for the creative process, be it the photographer, graphic designer, layout artist, or printer. Adobe is the Publishing and Imaging Software Partner for *America 24/7* and products such as Adobe InDesign®, Photoshop, Acrobat®, and Illustrator® were used to produce this stunning book in a matter of weeks. We hope that our software has helped do justice to the mythic images, contributed by well-known photographers and the inspired hobbyist.

Adobe is proud to be a lead sponsor of *America 24/7*, a project that celebrates the vibrancy of the American spirit: the same spirit that helped found Adobe and inspires our employees and customers to deliver the very best.

Bruce Chizen
President and CEO
Adobe Systems Incorporated

OLYMPUS

Olympus, a global technology leader in designing precision healthcare solutions and innovative consumer electronics, is proud to be the official digital camera sponsor of *America 24/7*. The opportunity to introduce Americans from coast to coast to the thrill, excitement, and possibility of digital photography makes the vision behind this book a perfect fit for Olympus, a leader in digital cameras since 1996.

For most people, the essence of digital photography is best grasped through firsthand experience with the technology, which is precisely what *America 24/7* is about. We understand that direct experience is the pathway to inspiration, and welcome opportunities like this sponsorship to bring the power of the digital experience into the lives of people everywhere. To Olympus, *America 24/7* offers a platform to help realize a core mission: to deliver and make accessible the power of the digital experience to millions of American photographers, amateurs, and professionals alike.

The 1,000 professional photographers contracted to shoot on the America 24/7 project were all equipped with Olympus C-5050 digital cameras. Like all Olympus products, the C-5050 is offered by a company well known for designing, manufacturing, and servicing products used by professionals to perform their work, every day. Olympus is a customer-centric company committed to working one-to-one with a diverse group of professionals. From biomedical researchers who use our clinical microscopes, to doctors who perform life-saving procedures with our endoscopes, to professional photographers who use cameras in their daily work, Olympus is a trusted brand.

The digital imaging technology involved with *America 24/7* has enabled the soul of America to be visually conveyed, not just by professional observers, but by the American public who participated in this project—the very people who collectively breath life into this country's existence each day.

We are proud to be enabling so many photographers to capture the pictures on these pages that tell the story of who we are as a nation. From sea to shining sea, digital imagery allows us to connect to one another in ways we never dreamed possible.

At Olympus, our ideas have proliferated as rapidly as technology has evolved. We have channeled these visions into breakthrough products and solutions to meet the demands of our changing world-products like microscopes, endoscopes, and digital voice recorders, supported by the highly regarded training, educational, and consulting services we offer our customers.

Today, 83 years after we introduced our first microscope, we remain as young, as curious, and as committed as ever.

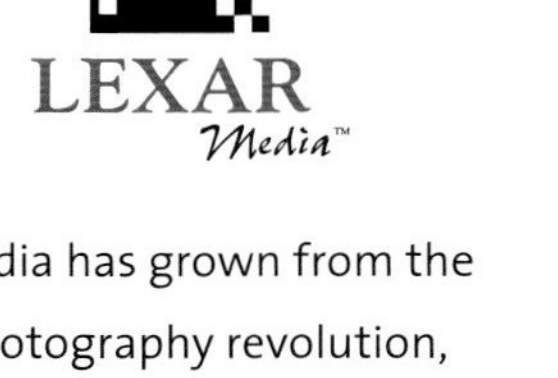

Lexar Media has grown from the digital photography revolution, which is why we are proud to have supplied the digital memory cards used in the America 24/7 project. Lexar Media's high-performance memory cards utilize our unique and patented controller coupled with high-speed flash memory from Samsung, the world's largest flash memory supplier. This powerful combination brings out the ultimate performance of any digital camera.

Photographers who demand the most from their equipment choose our products for their advanced features like write speeds up to 40X, Write Acceleration technology for enabled cameras, and Image Rescue, which recovers previously deleted or lost images. Leading camera manufacturers bundle Lexar Media digital memory cards with their cameras because they value its performance and reliability.

Lexar Media is at the forefront of digital photography as it transforms picture-taking worldwide, and we will continue to be a leader with new and innovative solutions for professionals and amateurs alike.

Snapfish, which developed the technology behind the *America 24/7* amateur photo event, is a leading online photo service, with more than 5 million members and 100 million photos posted online. Snapfish enables both film and digital camera owners to share, print, and store their most important photo memories, at prices that cannot be equaled. Digital camera users upload photos into a password-protected online album for free. Users can also order film-quality prints on professional photographic paper for as low as 25¢. Film camera users get a full set of prints, plus online sharing and storage, for just $2.99 per roll.

Founded in 1995, eBay created a powerful platform for the sale of goods and services by a passionate community of individuals and businesses. On any given day, there are millions of items across thousands of categories for sale on eBay. eBay enables trade on a local, national and international basis with customized sites in markets around the world.

Through an array of services, such as its payment solution provider PayPal, eBay is enabling global e-commerce for an ever-growing online community.

JetBlue Airways is proud to be *America 24/7's* preferred carrier, flying photographers, photo editors, and organizers across the United States.

Winner of Condé Nast Traveler's Readers' Choice Awards for Best Domestic Airline 2002, JetBlue provides friendly service and low fares for travelers in 22 cities in nine states across America.

On behalf of JetBlue's 5,000 crew members, we're excited to be involved in this remarkable project, and for the opportunity to serve American travelers each and every day, coast to coast, 24/7.

DIGITAL POND

Digital Pond has been a leading creator of large graphic displays for museums, corporations, trade shows, retail environments and fine art since 1992.

We were proud to bring together our creative, print and display capabilities to produce signage and displays for mission control, critical retouching for numerous key images for the book, and art galleries for the New York Public Library and Bryant Park.

The Pond's team and SplashPic® Online service enabled us to nimbly design, produce and install over 200 large graphic panels in two NYC locations within the truly "24/7" production schedule of less than ten days.

WebWare Corporation is pleased to be a major sponsor of the America 24/7 project. We take pride in being part of a groundbreaking adventure that is stretching the boundaries—and the imagination—in digital photography, digital asset management, publishing, news, and global events.

Our ActiveMedia Enterprise™ digital asset management software is the "nerve center" of *America 24/7*, the central repository for managing, sharing, and collaborating on the project's photographs. From photo editors and book publishers to 24/7's media relations and marketing personnel, ActiveMedia provides the application support that links all facets of the project team to the content worldwide.

WebWare helps Global 2000 firms securely manage, reuse, and distribute media assets locally or globally. Its suite of ActiveMedia software products provide powerful media services platforms for integrating rich media into content management systems marketing and communication portals; web publishing systems; and e-commerce portals.

Google's mission is to organize the world's information and make it universally accessible and useful.

With our focus on plucking just the right answer from an ocean of data, we were naturally drawn to the America 24/7 project. The book you hold is a compendium of images of American life distilled from thousands of photographs and infinite possibilities. Are you looking for emotion? Narrative? Shadows? Light? It's all here, thanks to a multitude of photographers and writers creating links between you, the reader, and a sea of wonderful stories. We celebrate the connections that constitute the human experience and are pleased to help engender them. And we're pleased to have been a small part of this project, which captures the results of that interaction so vividly, so dynamically, and so dramatically.

Special thanks to additional contributors: FileMaker, Apple, Camera Bits, LaCie, Now Software, Preclick, Outpost Digital, Xerox, Microsoft, WoodWing Software, net-linx Publishing Solutions, and Radical Media. The Savoy Hotel, San Francisco; The Pan Pacific, San Francisco; Four Seasons Hotel, San Francisco; and The Queen Anne Hotel. Photography editing facilities were generously hosted by CNET Networks, Inc.

Participating Photographers

Coordinator: Pim Van Hemmen, Assistant Managing Editor for Photography, *The Star-Ledger*

Peter Ackerman, *Asbury Park Press*
James W. Anness
Mark Baran
Pam Brennan
Lisa Cogland
Aristide Economopoulos, *The Star-Ledger*
George Farrell
Najlah Feanny
Barry Fellman
Thomas E. Franklin
Sarah J. Glover, *The Philadelphia Inquirer*
Paul Goldfinger
Mark Greenberg, *WorldPictureNews*
Chod Lang
Scott Lituchy, *The Star-Ledger*
Ellie Markovitch, *The Herald News*
Dennis McDonald, *Burlington County Times*
Nicola A. Menzie
Amanda Miller
Ed Murray
Noah K. Murray
Danielle P. Richards
April Saul*
Shaul Schwarz, Corbis
Brian Smiga, Preclick
Mia Song, *The Star-Ledger*
Daryl Stone, *Asbury Park Press*
Chad Sutton
Akira Suwa, *The Philadelphia Inquirer*
Jason Towlen
David M Warren
Gerald S. Williams

*Pulitzer Prize winner

Thumbnail Picture Credits

Credits for thumbnail photographs are listed by the page number and are in order from left to right.

20 David M Warren
Najlah Feanny
Scott Lituchy, *The Star-Ledger*
Robin Kavanagh
Thomas E. Franklin
Najlah Feanny
Najlah Feanny

21 Najlah Feanny
Thomas E. Franklin
Thomas E. Franklin
Najlah Feanny
Thomas E. Franklin
Thomas E. Franklin
Thomas E. Franklin

24 Kat Cilento
April Saul
Dennis McDonald, *Burlington County Times*
April Saul
April Saul
Aristide Economopoulos, *The Star-Ledger*
April Saul

25 April Saul
April Saul
April Saul
Ellie Markovitch, *The Herald News*
April Saul
Najlah Feanny
Najlah Feanny

26 Daryl Stone, *Asbury Park Press*
Akira Suwa, *The Philadelphia Inquirer*
Akira Suwa, *The Philadelphia Inquirer*
Dennis McDonald, *Burlington County Times*
Akira Suwa, *The Philadelphia Inquirer*
Daryl Stone, *Asbury Park Press*
Sarah J. Glover, *The Philadelphia Inquirer*

27 Daryl Stone, *Asbury Park Press*
Jason Towlen
Dennis McDonald, *Burlington County Times*
Dennis McDonald, *Burlington County Times*
Jason Towlen
Sarah J. Glover, *The Philadelphia Inquirer*
Jason Towlen

28 Danielle P. Richards
Dennis McDonald, *Burlington County Times*
Brian Smiga, Preclick
James W. Anness
April Saul
Dennis McDonald, *Burlington County Times*
Ellie Markovitch, *The Herald News*

29 Danielle P. Richards
James W. Anness
Richard Bell
Dennis McDonald, *Burlington County Times*
Thomas E. Franklin
Vicki Valerio, *The Philadelphia Inquirer*
Ellie Markovitch, *The Herald News*

30 Peter Ackerman, *Asbury Park Press*
Peter Ackerman, *Asbury Park Press*
Ed Murray
Peter Ackerman, *Asbury Park Press*
Peter Ackerman, *Asbury Park Press*
Peter Ackerman, *Asbury Park Press*
Aaron M. Cohen

31 Peter Ackerman, *Asbury Park Press*
Peter Ackerman, *Asbury Park Press*
Peter Ackerman, *Asbury Park Press*
Peter Ackerman, *Asbury Park Press*
Peter Ackerman, *Asbury Park Press*
Robin Kavanagh
Peter Ackerman, *Asbury Park Press*

32 April Saul
David M Warren
David M Warren
David M Warren
David M Warren
David M Warren
David M Warren

33 David M Warren
David M Warren
David M Warren
Ellie Markovitch, *The Herald News*
Ellie Markovitch, *The Herald News*
Peter Ackerman, *Asbury Park Press*
David M Warren

34 Tiffany J. Ruocco
Najlah Feanny
Jason Towlen
Najlah Feanny
Jason Towlen
Jason Towlen
Jason Towlen

35 Jason Towlen
Jason Towlen
Daryl Stone, *Asbury Park Press*
Jason Towlen
Jason Towlen
Jason Towlen
Tiffany J. Ruocco

36 Peter Ackerman, *Asbury Park Press*
Mia Song, *The Star-Ledger*
Daryl Stone, *Asbury Park Press*
Gerald S. Williams
Daryl Stone, *Asbury Park Press*
Ellie Markovitch, *The Herald News*
Ed Catlett

37 Daryl Stone, *Asbury Park Press*
Mia Song, *The Star-Ledger*
April Saul
Jason Towlen
Ed Murray
Peter Ackerman, *Asbury Park Press*
Tiffany J. Ruocco

38 Brian Smiga, Preclick
Sarah J. Glover, *The Philadelphia Inquirer*
Jorge F. Larrea
Sarah J. Glover, *The Philadelphia Inquirer*
Dennis McDonald, *Burlington County Times*
David M Warren
Brian Smiga, Preclick

39 Ed Murray
Kathleen Duxbury Yeaw
Mark Hopkins
Sarah J. Glover, *The Philadelphia Inquirer*
Brian Smiga, Preclick
Thomas E. Franklin
Sarah J. Glover, *The Philadelphia Inquirer*

41 Daryl Stone, *Asbury Park Press*
Danielle P. Richards
Daryl Stone, *Asbury Park Press*
Daryl Stone, *Asbury Park Press*
David M Warren
Thomas E. Franklin
Scott Lituchy, *The Star-Ledger*

42 Shaul Schwarz, Corbis
Dennis McDonald, *Burlington County Times*
Aristide Economopoulos, *The Star-Ledger*
Dennis McDonald, *Burlington County Times*
Shaul Schwarz, Corbis
Ed Murray
Ed Catlett

43 Shaul Schwarz, Corbis
Ed Murray
Shaul Schwarz, Corbis
Dennis McDonald, *Burlington County Times*
Peter Ackerman, *Asbury Park Press*
Shaul Schwarz, Corbis
James W. Anness

50 Akira Suwa, *The Philadelphia Inquirer*
James W. Anness
Akira Suwa, *The Philadelphia Inquirer*
James W. Anness
Akira Suwa, *The Philadelphia Inquirer*
James W. Anness
Rose Howerter

51 Akira Suwa, *The Philadelphia Inquirer*
James W. Anness
Ellie Markovitch, *The Herald News*
Akira Suwa, *The Philadelphia Inquirer*
James W. Anness
Sarah J. Glover, *The Philadelphia Inquirer*
James W. Anness

53 Peter Ackerman, *Asbury Park Press*
Peter Ackerman, *Asbury Park Press*
Peter Ackerman, *Asbury Park Press*
Peter Ackerman, *Asbury Park Press*
Peter Ackerman, *Asbury Park Press*
Peter Ackerman, *Asbury Park Press*
Peter Ackerman, *Asbury Park Press*

55 Peter Ackerman, *Asbury Park Press*
Peter Ackerman, *Asbury Park Press*
Peter Ackerman, *Asbury Park Press*
Peter Ackerman, *Asbury Park Press*
Peter Ackerman, *Asbury Park Press*
Peter Ackerman, *Asbury Park Press*
Peter Ackerman, *Asbury Park Press*

58 Danielle P. Richards
Scott Lituchy, *The Star-Ledger*
Danielle P. Richards
Danielle P. Richards
Danielle P. Richards
Danielle P. Richards
Scott Lituchy, *The Star-Ledger*

59 Scott Lituchy, *The Star-Ledger*
Scott Lituchy, *The Star-Ledger*
Danielle P. Richards
Scott Lituchy, *The Star-Ledger*
Scott Lituchy, *The Star-Ledger*
Thomas E. Franklin
Danielle P. Richards

62 Daryl Stone, *Asbury Park Press*
Ed Murray
Ellie Markovitch, *The Herald News*
James W. Anness
James W. Anness
Jorge F. Larrea
James W. Anness

63 Daryl Stone, *Asbury Park Press*
James W. Anness
James W. Anness
Daryl Stone, *Asbury Park Press*
James W. Anness
Thomas E. Franklin
James W. Anness

66 Aristide Economopoulos, *The Star-Ledger*
Aristide Economopoulos, *The Star-Ledger*
Aristide Economopoulos, *The Star-Ledger*
Aristide Economopoulos, *The Star-Ledger*
Aristide Economopoulos, *The Star-Ledger*
Aristide Economopoulos, *The Star-Ledger*
Sarah J. Glover, *The Philadelphia Inquirer*

67 Ellie Markovitch, *The Herald News*
Ellie Markovitch, *The Herald News*
Daryl Stone, *Asbury Park Press*
Aristide Economopoulos, *The Star-Ledger*
Aristide Economopoulos, *The Star-Ledger*
Sarah J. Glover, *The Philadelphia Inquirer*
Aristide Economopoulos, *The Star-Ledger*

68 Aristide Economopoulos, *The Star-Ledger*
Thomas E. Franklin
Ed Murray
Daryl Stone, *Asbury Park Press*
Thomas E. Franklin
Kathleen Duxbury Yeaw
Thomas E. Franklin

69 Ed Murray
Daryl Stone, *Asbury Park Press*
Thomas E. Franklin
Ed Murray
Ed Murray
Thomas E. Franklin
Thomas E. Franklin

70 Ellie Markovitch, *The Herald News*
James W. Anness
Rose Howerter
James W. Anness
Danielle P. Richards
James W. Anness
James W. Anness

71 Ellie Markovitch, *The Herald News*
James W. Anness
Jorge F. Larrea
James W. Anness
James W. Anness
Rose Howerter
Thomas E. Franklin

74 April Saul
April Saul
April Saul
April Saul
April Saul
David M Warren
April Saul

75 April Saul
April Saul
Sarah J. Glover, *The Philadelphia Inquirer*
Sarah J. Glover, *The Philadelphia Inquirer*
April Saul
Sarah J. Glover, *The Philadelphia Inquirer*
Sarah J. Glover, *The Philadelphia Inquirer*

76 Najlah Feanny
Paul J. Buklarewicz
Paul J. Buklarewicz
Thomas E. Franklin
Najlah Feanny
Scott Lituchy, *The Star-Ledger*
Najlah Feanny

77 Paul J. Buklarewicz
Scott Lituchy, *The Star-Ledger*
Thomas E. Franklin
Najlah Feanny
Aristide Economopoulos, *The Star-Ledger*
Scott Lituchy, *The Star-Ledger*
Paul J. Buklarewicz

80 Brian Smiga, Preclick
Ed Murray
Scott Lituchy, *The Star-Ledger*
Sarah J. Glover, *The Philadelphia Inquirer*
Noah K. Murray
Scott Lituchy, *The Star-Ledger*
Ed Catlett

85 Akira Suwa, *The Philadelphia Inquirer*
Aristide Economopoulos, *The Star-Ledger*
Ed Murray
Ed Murray
Ed Murray
Ed Murray
Ed Murray

87 Aristide Economopoulos, *The Star-Ledger*
Aristide Economopoulos, *The Star-Ledger*
Aristide Economopoulos, *The Star-Ledger*
Daryl Stone, *Asbury Park Press*
Aristide Economopoulos, *The Star-Ledger*
Aristide Economopoulos, *The Star-Ledger*
Aristide Economopoulos, *The Star-Ledger*

90 Brian Smiga, Preclick
Brian Smiga, Preclick
Ed Murray
Ed Murray
Brian Smiga, Preclick
Ed Murray
Daryl Stone, *Asbury Park Press*

91 Ed Murray
Ed Murray
Ellie Markovitch, *The Herald News*
Thomas E. Franklin
Ed Murray
Ellie Markovitch, *The Herald News*
Thomas E. Franklin

96 Akira Suwa, *The Philadelphia Inquirer*
Barry Fellman
Scott Lituchy, *The Star-Ledger*
Scott Lituchy, *The Star-Ledger*
Akira Suwa, *The Philadelphia Inquirer*
Scott Lituchy, *The Star-Ledger*
Scott Lituchy, *The Star-Ledger*

97 Eric Mencher
Akira Suwa, *The Philadelphia Inquirer*
Scott Lituchy, *The Star-Ledger*
Akira Suwa, *The Philadelphia Inquirer*
Scott Lituchy, *The Star-Ledger*
Scott Lituchy, *The Star-Ledger*
Daryl Stone, *Asbury Park Press*

100 Gerald S. Williams
Mark Greenberg, WorldPictureNews
Gerald S. Williams
Danielle P. Richards
Mark Greenberg, WorldPictureNews
Danielle P. Richards
Mark Greenberg, WorldPictureNews

101 Mark Greenberg, WorldPictureNews
April Saul
Mark Greenberg, WorldPictureNews
Mark Greenberg, WorldPictureNews
Mark Greenberg, WorldPictureNews
Mark Greenberg, WorldPictureNews
Danielle P. Richards

104 April Saul
Daryl Stone, *Asbury Park Press*
Sarah J. Glover, *The Philadelphia Inquirer*
Ed Murray
Sarah J. Glover, *The Philadelphia Inquirer*
Ed Murray
Daryl Stone, *Asbury Park Press*

105 Mia Song, *The Star-Ledger*
Jason Towlen
Paul J. Buklarewicz
Sarah J. Glover, *The Philadelphia Inquirer*
April Saul
Paul J. Buklarewicz
Jason Towlen

107 Peter Ackerman, *Asbury Park Press*
Peter Ackerman, *Asbury Park Press*
Peter Ackerman, *Asbury Park Press*
Peter Ackerman, *Asbury Park Press*
Peter Ackerman, *Asbury Park Press*
Peter Ackerman, *Asbury Park Press*
Peter Ackerman, *Asbury Park Press*

108 Peter Ackerman, *Asbury Park Press*
Aaron M. Cohen
Peter Ackerman, *Asbury Park Press*
Peter Ackerman, *Asbury Park Press*
Peter Ackerman, *Asbury Park Press*
Aaron M. Cohen
Peter Ackerman, *Asbury Park Press*

109 Aristide Economopoulos, *The Star-Ledger*
Peter Ackerman, *Asbury Park Press*
Peter Ackerman, *Asbury Park Press*
Sarah J. Glover, *The Philadelphia Inquirer*
Peter Ackerman, *Asbury Park Press*
Aristide Economopoulos, *The Star-Ledger*
Peter Ackerman, *Asbury Park Press*

110 Brian Smiga, Preclick
Daryl Stone, *Asbury Park Press*
Brian Smiga, Preclick
Daryl Stone, *Asbury Park Press*
Daryl Stone, *Asbury Park Press*
Daryl Stone, *Asbury Park Press*
Daryl Stone, *Asbury Park Press*

111 Daryl Stone, *Asbury Park Press*
Barry Fellman
Najlah Feanny
Daryl Stone, *Asbury Park Press*
Daryl Stone, *Asbury Park Press*
Daryl Stone, *Asbury Park Press*
Daryl Stone, *Asbury Park Press*

114 Barry Fellman
Brian Smiga, Preclick
Barry Fellman
Scott Lituchy, *The Star-Ledger*
Ed Murray
Ellie Markovitch, *The Herald News*
Scott Lituchy, *The Star-Ledger*

115 Karen Labenz
Scott Lituchy, *The Star-Ledger*
Barry Fellman
Scott Lituchy, *The Star-Ledger*
Scott Lituchy, *The Star-Ledger*
Scott Lituchy, *The Star-Ledger*
Scott Lituchy, *The Star-Ledger*

116 Akira Suwa, *The Philadelphia Inquirer*
Dennis McDonald, *Burlington County Times*
Daryl Stone, *Asbury Park Press*
Vicki Valerio, *The Philadelphia Inquirer*
Dennis McDonald, *Burlington County Times*
Paul J. Buklarewicz
Kathleen Duxbury Yeaw

118 Akira Suwa, *The Philadelphia Inquirer*
Nicola A. Menzie
April Saul
Akira Suwa, *The Philadelphia Inquirer*
April Saul
Nicola A. Menzie
April Saul

119 Akira Suwa, *The Philadelphia Inquirer*
Greg Walls
Nicola A. Menzie
Najlah Feanny
Nicola A. Menzie
Noah K. Murray
Greg Walls

122 Aaron M. Cohen
Aristide Economopoulos, *The Star-Ledger*
Ed Murray
Aristide Economopoulos, *The Star-Ledger*
Ed Murray
Peter Ackerman, *Asbury Park Press*
Ed Murray

123 Peter Ackerman, *Asbury Park Press*
Keith Dillon
Peter Ackerman, *Asbury Park Press*
Keith Dillon
Peter Ackerman, *Asbury Park Press*
Peter Ackerman, *Asbury Park Press*
Sarah J. Glover, *The Philadelphia Inquirer*

124 David M Warren
April Saul
Barry Fellman
April Saul
April Saul
Brian Smiga, Preclick
April Saul

125 David M Warren
Sarah J. Glover, *The Philadelphia Inquirer*
Daryl Stone, *Asbury Park Press*
April Saul
Thomas E. Franklin
Sarah J. Glover, *The Philadelphia Inquirer*
Thomas E. Franklin

126 Ed Murray
Shaul Schwarz, Corbis
Ed Murray
Ed Murray
Ed Murray
Shaul Schwarz, Corbis
Keith Dillon

128 Jorge F. Larrea
Ed Murray
Ed Murray
Aristide Economopoulos, *The Star-Ledger*
Ed Murray
Ed Murray
Thomas E. Franklin

129 Ed Catlett
Ed Murray
Ed Murray
Dennis McDonald, *Burlington County Times*
Daryl Stone, *Asbury Park Press*
David Scull, Apix
Dennis McDonald, *Burlington County Times*

132 Kathleen Duxbury Yeaw
Brian Smiga, Preclick
Ed Murray
Dennis McDonald, *Burlington County Times*
Dennis McDonald, *Burlington County Times*
Paul J. Buklarewicz
Mark Hopkins

133 Jorge F. Larrea
Dennis McDonald, *Burlington County Times*
Thomas E. Franklin
Dennis McDonald, *Burlington County Times*
Brian Smiga, Preclick
Thomas E. Franklin
Thomas E. Franklin

Staff

The *America 24/7* series was imagined years ago by our friend Oscar Dystel, a publishing legend whose vision and enthusiasm have been a source of great inspiration.

We also wish to express our gratitude to our truly visionary publisher, DK.

Rick Smolan, Project Director
David Elliot Cohen, Project Director

Administrative
Katya Able, Operations Director
Gina Privitere, Communications Director
Chuck Gathard, Technology Director
Kim Shannon, Photographer Relations Director
Erin O'Connor, Photographer Relations Intern
Leslie Hunter, Partnership Director
Annie Polk, Publicity Manager
John McAlester, Website Manager
Alex Notides, Office Manager
C. Thomas Hardin, State Photography Coordinator

Design
Brad Zucroff, Creative Director
Karen Mullarkey, Photography Director
Judy Zimola, Production Manager
David Simoni, Production Designer
Mary Dias, Production Designer
Heidi Madison, Associate Picture Editor
Don McCartney, Production Designer
Diane Dempsey Murray, Production Designer
Jan Rogers, Associate Picture Editor
Bill Shore, Production Designer and Image Artist
Larry Nighswander, Senior Picture Editor
Bill Marr, Sarah Leen, Senior Picture Editors
Peter Truskier, Workflow Consultant
Jim Birkenseer, Workflow Consultant

Editorial
Maggie Canon, Managing Editor
Curt Sanburn, Senior Editor
Teresa L. Trego, Production Editor
Lea Aschkenas, Writer
Olivia Boler, Writer
Korey Capozza, Writer
Beverly Hanly, Writer
Bridgett Novak, Writer
Alison Owings, Writer
Fred Raker, Writer
Joe Wolff, Writer
Elise O'Keefe, Copy Chief
Daisy Hernández, Copy Editor
Jennifer Wolfe, Copy Editor

Infographic Design
Nigel Holmes

Literary Agent
Carol Mann, The Carol Mann Agency

Legal Counsel
Barry Reder, Coblentz, Patch, Duffy & Bass, LLP
Phil Feldman, Coblentz, Patch, Duffy & Bass, LLP
Gabe Perle, Ohlandt, Greeley, Ruggiero & Perle, LLP
Jon Hart, Dow, Lohnes & Albertson, PLLC
Mike Hays, Dow, Lohnes & Albertson, PLLC
Stephen Pollen, Warshaw Burstein, Cohen, Schlesinger & Kuh, LLP
Rick Pappas

Accounting and Finance
Rita Dulebohn, Accountant
Robert Powers, Calegari, Morris & Co. Accountants
Eugene Blumberg, Blumberg & Associates
Arthur Langhaus, KLS Professional Advisors Group, Inc.

Picture Editors
J. David Ake, Associated Press
Caren Alpert, formerly *Health* magazine
Simon Barnett, *Newsweek*
Caroline Couig, *San Jose Mercury News*
Mike Davis, formerly *National Geographic*
Michel duCille, *Washington Post*
Deborah Dragon, *Rolling Stone*
Victor Fisher, formerly Associated Press
Frank Folwell, *USA Today*
MaryAnne Golon, *Time*
Liz Grady, formerly *National Geographic*
Randall Greenwell, *San Francisco Chronicle*
C. Thomas Hardin, formerly *Louisville Courier-Journal*
Kathleen Hennessy, *San Francisco Chronicle*
Scot Jahn, *U.S. News & World Report*
Steve Jessmore, *Flint Journal*
John Kaplan, University of Florida
Kim Komenich, *San Francisco Chronicle*
Eliane Laffont, *Hachette Filipacchi Media*
Jean-Pierre Laffont, *Hachette Filipacchi Media*
Andrew Locke, MSNBC
Jose Lopez, *The New York Times*
Maria Mann, formerly AFP
Bill Marr, formerly *National Geographic*
Michele McNally, *Fortune*
James Merithew, *San Francisco Chronicle*
Eric Meskauskas, *New York Daily News*
Maddy Miller, *People* magazine
Michelle Molloy, *Newsweek*
Dolores Morrison, *New York Daily News*
Karen Mullarkey, formerly *Newsweek, Rolling Stone, Sports Illustrated*
Larry Nighswander, Ohio University School of Visual Communication
Jim Preston, *Baltimore Sun*
Sarah Rozen, formerly *Entertainment Weekly*
Mike Smith, *The New York Times*
Neal Ulevich, formerly Associated Press

Website and Digital Systems
Jeff Burchell, Applications Engineer

Television Documentary
Sandy Smolan, Producer/Director
Rick King, Producer/Director
Bill Medsker, Producer

Video News Release
Mike Cerre, Producer/Director

Digital Pond
Peter Hogg
Kris Knight
Roger Graham
Philip Bond
Frank De Pace
Lisa Li

Senior Advisors
Jennifer Erwitt, Strategic Advisor
Tom Walker, Creative Advisor
Megan Smith, Technology Advisor
Jon Kamen, Media and Partnership Advisor
Mark Greenberg, Partnership Advisor
Patti Richards, Publicity Advisor
Cotton Coulson, Mission Control Advisor

Executive Advisors
Sonia Land
George Craig
Carole Bidnick

Advisors
Chris Anderson
Samir Arora
Russell Brown
Craig Cline
Gayle Cline
Harlan Felt
George Fisher
Phillip Moffitt
Clement Mok
Laureen Seeger
Richard Saul Wurman

DK Publishing
Bill Barry
Joanna Bull
Therese Burke
Sarah Coltman
Christopher Davis
Todd Fries
Dick Heffernan
Jay Henry
Stuart Jackman
Stephanie Jackson
Chuck Lang
Sharon Lucas
Cathy Melnicki
Nicola Munro
Eunice Paterson
Andrew Welham

Colourscan
Jimmy Tsao
Eddie Chia
Richard Law
Josephine Yam
Paul Koh
Chee Cheng Yeong
Dan Kang

Chief Morale Officer
Goose, the dog

ALABAMA24/7
ALASKA24/7
ARIZONA24/7
ARKANSAS24/7
CALIFORNIA24/7
HAWAII24/7
IDAHO24/7
ILLINOIS24/7
INDIANA24/7
IOWA24/7
MASSACHUSETTS24/7
MICHIGAN24/7
MINNESOTA24/7
MISSISSIPPI24/7
MISSOURI24/7
NEW MEXICO24/7
NEW YORK24/7
NORTH CAROLINA24/7
NORTH DAKOTA24/7
OHIO24/7
SOUTH DAKOTA24/7
TENNESSEE24/7
TEXAS24/7
UTAH24/7
VERMONT24/7
Amazing Photographs of An Extraordinary State.
DK